P O C K E T S

SHARKS

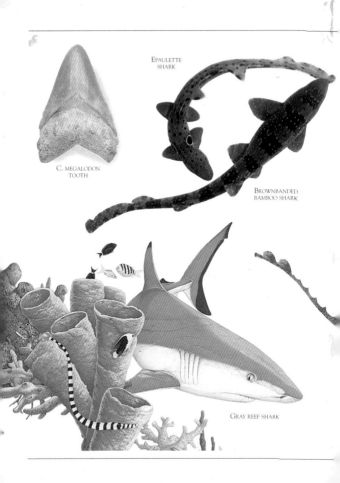

EPAULETTE
SHARK

C. MEGALODON
TOOTH

BROWNBANDED
BAMBOO SHARK

GRAY REEF SHARK

P O C K E T S
SHARKS

Written by
JOYCE POPE

THRESHER
SHARK

RAY

HAMMERHEAD
SHARK

DK PUBLISHING

LONDON, NEW YORK,
MELBOURNE, MUNICH, and DELHI

Project editor Anna McMurray
Art editors Martin Wilson, Jacqui Burton
Design assistant Tanya Tween
Senior editor Alastair Dougall
Senior art editors Carole Oliver, Sarah Crouch
Picture research Neil Aldridge
Production Kate Oliver
US Editor Irene Pavitt

REVISED EDITION
Project editor Steve Setford
Designer Sarah Crouch
Managing editor Linda Esposito
Managing art editor Jane Thomas
DTP designer Siu Yin Ho
Consultant Rolf Williams
Production Erica Rosen
US editors Margaret Parrish, Christine Heilman

016-PD039-July/2003

Second American Edition, 2003
Published in the United States by
DK Publishing, Inc., 375 Hudson Street,
New York, New York 10014

11 12 13 14 13 12 11 10

Copyright © 2003 Dorling Kindersley Limited

A Cataloging-in-Publication record for the First American Edition of this book
is available from the Library of Congress.

ISBN-13: 978-0-7894-9592-1

Color reproduction by Colourscan, Singapore
Printed in China

See our complete product line at
www.dk.com

CONTENTS

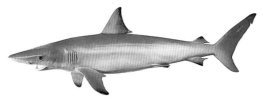

HOW TO USE THIS BOOK

These pages show you how to use *Pockets: Sharks*.
The book is divided into five sections. The first four
provide information about the anatomy, behavior,
and the different species of sharks. The last section
contains a classification table, followed by a glossary
and a comprehensive index.

ALL ABOUT SHARKS
This book has been
divided into five sections.
Turn to the contents
pages, index, or glossary
for more information
about anatomy, types of
species, behavior, or the
role of sharks in science
and conservation.

CORNER CODING
The corners of the
main section pages are
color coded to
remind you which
section you are in.

- ANATOMY
- LIVING AND SURVIVING
- SHARKS AND HUMANS
- SHARK DIRECTORY
- SHARKS FOR THE FUTURE

Corner coding

Heading

Introduction

LIVING AND SURVIVING

FEEDING HABITS

SHARKS EAT MANY different types of food, but all are
flesh-eaters. Most eat small fish or invertebrates and
some will grab carrion when they can. Three large
species filter food, known as plankton, from the sea.
Some sharks hunt large animals, including sea lions
and other sharks.

GENTLE G
The whal
shark o
feeds on
plankton.
Meshlike fil
soft tiny creat
from the wate
passes over it.
On occasion th
whale shark ha
an active homin
preying on shoa
of small fish, su
as anchovy.

FEEDING FACTS
- Sharks do not need
to feed every day.
- Undigested food may
remain in the stomach
for several days.
- Smell and the lateral
line are the principal
senses used by the
shark to lead it to food.

SHARP TEETH
The horn shark uses its
sense of smell to locate
animals such as sea
urchins and shellfish
on which it feeds.
They are caught
with its sharp front
teeth and crushed
with flat teeth in the
back of its mouth.

Fact box   *Annotation*

HEADING
The heading
describes the
subject of the page.
This page is about
the feeding habits
and tooth shapes
of various sharks.

INTRODUCTION
The introduction
provides an overview
of the subject. After
reading this, you
should have a clear
idea of what the pages
are about.

LABELS
For extra clarity, some
pictures have labels. A
label identifies a picture
if it is not immediately
obvious what it is from
the text.

RUNNING HEADS

These remind you which section you are in. The top of the left-hand page gives the section name, and the top of the right-hand page gives the subject heading. The page on feeding habits is from the Living and Surviving section.

FACT BOXES

Many pages have fact boxes. These provide at-a-glance information about a subject, such as how long undigested food can remain in the stomach, and what senses the shark uses to lead it to food.

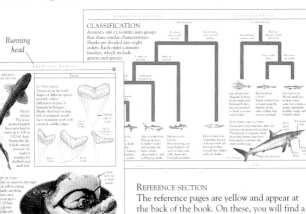

Running head

Caption

Label

CAPTIONS AND ANNOTATIONS

Each illustration carries an explanatory caption. Some also have annotations, in *italics*. These point out the features of an illustration, and often use leader lines.

REFERENCE SECTION

The reference pages are yellow and appear at the back of the book. On these, you will find a classification table, and other interesting facts and records about sharks. There is a list of conservation organizations and aquariums on the resources pages.

INDEX

At the back of the book is an index listing every subject in the book. By referring to the index, information on particular topics can be found quickly. A glossary defines the technical terms used in the book.

INTRODUCTION

ABOUT SHARKS

SHARKS ARE SHY, elusive creatures. Even though they spend little time at the surface and are rarely seen, sharks roam all the world's oceans. Anyone who has swum in the sea has almost certainly been close to sharks. All sharks are flesh-eaters, but humans are not part of their natural diet.

HAMMERHEAD
Sharks are generally solitary creatures, but sharks such as spiny dogfish, blue sharks, and the scalloped hammerhead shark swim in groups.

The great white may lift its head out of the water to inspect surface objects

Pointed snout

Light-colored underbelly

GREAT WHITE
There are more than 400 species of sharks. The most feared is the great white or white pointer, which lives near the surface of temperate and tropical seas. Its main food is large fish, turtles, and seals. While hunting seals, the great white will occasionally attack humans by mistake.

Pectoral fin

ONE-YEAR-OLD
LEOPARD SHARK

SHARK SPOTS
The leopard shark gets its name from its spotted skin. Its teeth have rounded tops for crushing the hard-shelled creatures, such as clams and sea snails, on which it feeds. This shark is frequently kept in marine aquariums since it adapts well to captivity.

This shark is 15 in (38 cm) in length

HORN SHARK
The horn shark is a slow, bottom-living species. It feeds on hard-shelled prey and is harmless unless disturbed. It lays spiral-shaped egg cases, which it wedges into crevices in rocks to keep them safe from enemies until they hatch.

Spotted pattern on skin

Pelvic fin

SHARK EATS MUM ALIVE AS KIDS WATCH

by IAN HEPBURN

A MOTHER of five was bitten in two by a 13ft shark while her children watched in horror from a boat.

Horror on dive at nature spot

NEWS SENSATION
A human stands little chance in an encounter with a large shark, as this attack in Australia demonstrates. Shark attacks always make the headlines. They often take place close to land in shallow water, where children play and most people swim.

THE SHARK'S DOMAIN

THE WORLD'S OCEANS are the shark's domain. A few species, such as the blue shark, are found throughout the warmer parts of this vast area, but many are restricted to certain coasts or to types of watery habitat, such as muddy bays or the edges of coral reefs. The majority live in the well-lit surface zone, but others are found in very deep water.

SEA HOME
Nurse sharks are often found where the sea is shallow. On the outer side of a reef, where the water is deeper, species such as the blacktip reef shark abound. The blue shark and the great white, both fast-swimming hunters, and the slow-moving, huge whale shark are most often seen in the open seas. The strange-looking lantern and goblin shark live in the depths of the ocean.

Continental shelf

Continental slope

Blacktip reef shark

FRESHWATER EXPLORERS
Bull sharks inhabit tropical rivers and lakes as well as the sea. They have been spotted 2,298 miles (3,700 km) from the sea in the Amazon River. They are a great danger to other river dwellers.

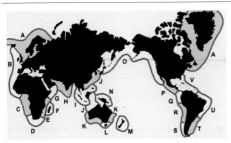

WORLD MAP
This map shows the distribution of some coastal-living sharks. While many sharks are found throughout the world, the examples shown here demonstrate that some shark species are restricted to particular areas.

A. Greenland shark
B. Portuguese dogfish
C. African lantern shark
D. Sharptooth houndshark
E. Thorny lantern shark
F. Blue-spotted bamboo shark
G. Smallbelly catshark

H. Slender bamboo shark
I. Brown-spotted catshark
J. Zebra bullhead shark
K. Port Jackson shark
L. Dumb gulper shark
M. Plunket shark
N. Tassled wobbegong

O. Pacific sleeper shark
P. Whitenose shark
Q. Panama ghost shark
R. Hooktooth dogfish
S. Dusky catshark
T. Argentine angel shark
U. Freckled catshark
V. Caribbean reef shark

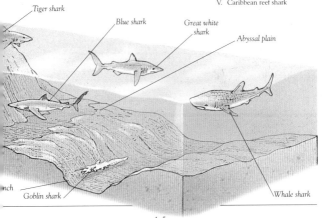

Tiger shark

Blue shark

Great white shark

Abyssal plain

nch

Goblin shark

Whale shark

EARLY EVIDENCE

THE TEETH of sharks are common fossils. The first sharks lived about 380 million years ago, in a sea that covered what is now Ohio. When they died, they sank so quickly into the silt on the seabed that their skeletons are well preserved.

SPIRAL FOSSIL TEETH
Unlike other sharks, *Helicoprion* retained its teeth in its upper and lower jaws, rather than shedding them at regular intervals. The oldest teeth are in the middle of the spiral.

Diameter of teeth whorl is about 6.5 in (17 cm)

Teeth were constantly pushed back, forming a spiral

HELICOPRION
Scientists are unsure exactly what *Helicoprion* looked like, or fed on, since only its teeth have ever been found. This shark survived for nearly 100 million years but left no descendants. Its fossils are widespread throughout the world.

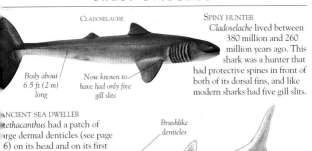

CLADOSELACHE

SPINY HUNTER
Cladoselache lived between 380 million and 260 million years ago. This shark was a hunter that had protective spines in front of both of its dorsal fins, and like modern sharks had five gill slits.

Body about 6.5 ft (2 m) long

Now known to have had only five gill slits

ANCIENT SEA DWELLER
...tethacanthus had a patch of ...rge dermal denticles (see page ...6) on its head and on its first ...orsal fin. They may have been ...r protection, ... enabled ... to latch ...n to bigger ...sh, just as ...he modern ...emora does.

Brushlike denticles

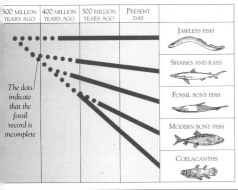

Anal fin

Clasper

500 MILLION YEARS AGO	400 MILLION YEARS AGO	300 MILLION YEARS AGO	PRESENT DAY	
				JAWLESS FISH
				SHARKS AND RAYS
				FOSSIL BONY FISH
				MODERN BONY FISH
				COELACANTHS

The dots indicate that the fossil record is incomplete

FISH EVOLUTION
Fish have lived in the sea for nearly 500 million years. The first fish were jawless, like lampreys. Modern fish appeared at the end of the Age of Dionosaurs, about 65 million years ago. *Coelacanth* and sturgeons have survived the extinction of most of their relatives.

1 7

ANCIENT SHARKS

SINCE THE FIRST SHARKS evolved, ways of
life in the sea have changed very little.
As a result, many of today's sharks are
much like their ancient ancestors –
some are so similar that
people think of them as
living fossils. As such they
can tell us a great deal about
animals that may
have been extinct
for many millions
of years.

PORT JACKSON
SHARK

OLD RELATIVE
Fossils of fish
very similar to
the Port Jackson
shark have been found in rocks 150 million
years old. They fed on hard-shelled prey such as
oysters and clams, which they crushed with
strangely shaped, ridged teeth.

ELUSIVE
SPECIES
The frilled
shark lives in
deeper water than many other
species and remained unknown
to science until the late 19th
century. Unusual-looking on
the outside, it is even
stranger under the skin, for some
parts of its skeleton resemble those of sharks
that became extinct 350 million years ago.

FRILLED
SHARK

Eel-shaped
body

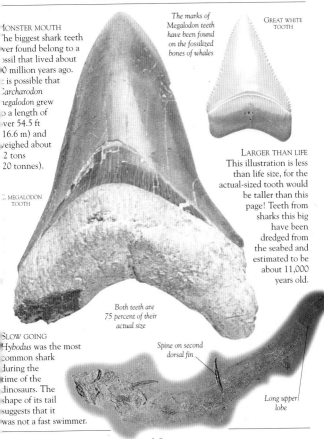

MONSTER MOUTH
The biggest shark teeth
ever found belong to a
fossil that lived about
10 million years ago.
It is possible that
Carcharodon
megalodon grew
to a length of
over 54.5 ft
(16.6 m) and
weighed about
22 tons
(20 tonnes).

C. MEGALODON
TOOTH

*The marks of
Megalodon teeth
have been found
on the fossilized
bones of whales*

GREAT WHITE
TOOTH

LARGER THAN LIFE
This illustration is less
than life size, for the
actual-sized tooth would
be taller than this
page! Teeth from
sharks this big
have been
dredged from
the seabed and
estimated to be
about 11,000
years old.

*Both teeth are
75 percent of their
actual size*

SLOW GOING
Hybodus was the most
common shark
during the
time of the
dinosaurs. The
shape of its tail
suggests that it
was not a fast swimmer.

*Spine on second
dorsal fin*

*Long upper
lobe*

CLOSE RELATIVES

IT IS HARD TO BELIEVE that flat, slow-moving skates and rays, which live on the bed of the sea, are related to fast, streamlined sharks. However, rays' and sharks' anatomy is very similar: for example, both have cartilaginous skeletons (see page 34) and up to seven gill slits.

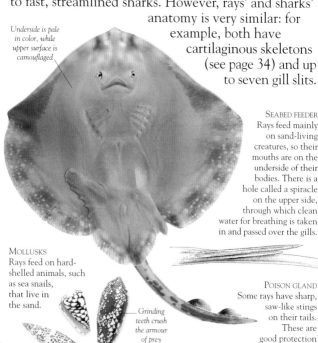

Underside is pale in color, while upper surface is camouflaged

SEABED FEEDER
Rays feed mainly on sand-living creatures, so their mouths are on the underside of their bodies. There is a hole called a spiracle on the upper side, through which clean water for breathing is taken in and passed over the gills.

MOLLUSKS
Rays feed on hard-shelled animals, such as sea snails, that live in the sand.

Grinding teeth crush the armour of prey

POISON GLAND
Some rays have sharp, saw-like stings on their tails. These are good protection against their enemies.

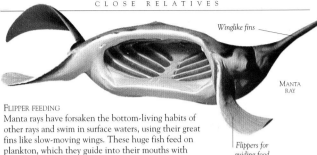

Winglike fins

MANTA
RAY

*Flippers for
guiding food*

FLIPPER FEEDING
Manta rays have forsaken the bottom-living habits of
other rays and swim in surface waters, using their great
fins like slow-moving wings. These huge fish feed on
plankton, which they guide into their mouths with
flipperlike organs on either side of their heads.

SUN BATHER
The pygmy devil ray is smaller than
the great manta. In warm seas, it can
sometimes be seen lying on the surface,
before leaping out of the water
and speeding away.

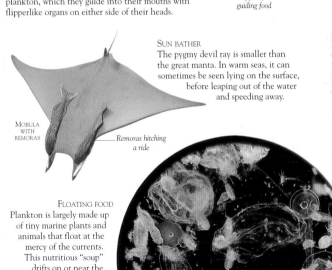

MOBULA
WITH
REMORAS

*Remoras hitching
a ride*

FLOATING FOOD
Plankton is largely made up
of tiny marine plants and
animals that float at the
mercy of the currents.
This nutritious "soup"
drifts on or near the
surface of the sea.

ANATOMY

NOSE TO TAIL

MOST SHARKS are large fish, designed for constant, effortless swimming, though not at sustained high speeds. Their color is usually a bluish gray, to blend with the colors of the ocean. Their senses, like their teeth, are razor-sharp, and they are quick to investigate anything that could be food.

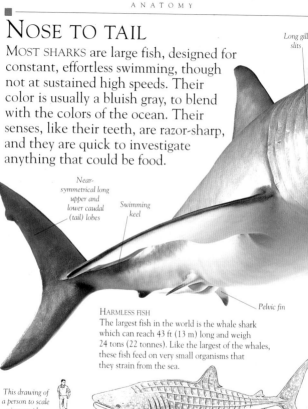

Long gill slits

Near-symmetrical long upper and lower caudal (tail) lobes

Swimming keel

Pelvic fin

HARMLESS FISH
The largest fish in the world is the whale shark which can reach 43 ft (13 m) long and weigh 24 tons (22 tonnes). Like the largest of the whales, these fish feed on very small organisms that they strain from the sea.

This drawing of a person to scale gives an idea of the whale shark's large size

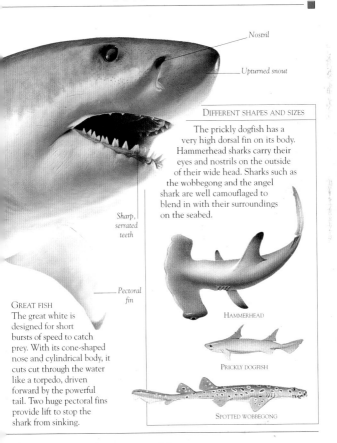

Nostril

Upturned snout

DIFFERENT SHAPES AND SIZES

The prickly dogfish has a very high dorsal fin on its body. Hammerhead sharks carry their eyes and nostrils on the outside of their wide head. Sharks such as the wobbegong and the angel shark are well camouflaged to blend in with their surroundings on the seabed.

Sharp, serrated teeth

Pectoral fin

GREAT FISH
The great white is designed for short bursts of speed to catch prey. With its cone-shaped nose and cylindrical body, it cuts cut through the water like a torpedo, driven forward by the powerful tail. Two huge pectoral fins provide lift to stop the shark from sinking.

HAMMERHEAD

PRICKLY DOGFISH

SPOTTED WOBBEGONG

TAILS AND FINS

A SHARK PROPELS itself through the water by moving its powerful tail from side to side. The large, paired front fins provide lift, and can also act as brakes. The other, smaller fins give stability in the water. Unlike most fish, a shark's fins are supported internally by rods of cartilage, so they cannot be folded against the body.

SWIMMING AID
The shape of a shark's tail is important to the speed it can swim. Sharks with evenly balanced caudal fins (tails) are the fastest swimmers, whereas slower sharks may have hardly any lower lobe to their tail.

THRASHING TAIL
A thresher shark uses its tail to help it get food. Beating the water with the long upper lobe of its tail frightens and stuns small fish, making them easier to catch.

Enlarged upper caudal lobe

TAIL OF THRESHER SHARK

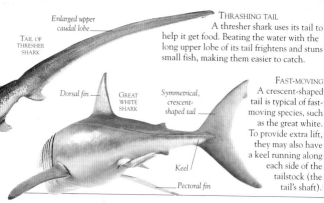

Dorsal fin

GREAT WHITE SHARK

Symmetrical, crescent-shaped tail

FAST-MOVING
A crescent-shaped tail is typical of fast-moving species, such as the great white. To provide extra lift, they may also have a keel running along each side of the tailstock (the tail's shaft).

Keel

Pectoral fin

UNIQUE TAIL
Angel sharks have
very large fins, which
make them look
like skates. Like
skates, they live on
the seabed, but they
swim like sharks, using
their slender tails and
not their fins for
propulsion. Unlike
most sharks, the lower
lobe of an angel
shark's tail is bigger
than the upper lobe.

SHAPELY TAIL
The swell shark, which
lives in kelp beds close
to the shore, has a tail
that is not designed for fast
swimming. In spite of this, the
swell shark is a very effective hunter
of small fish.

Anal fin

TAIL OF SWELL SHARK

SEABED
DWELLER
The horn
shark has large
fins and a small tail
for its size. Tagging
has shown that it
sometimes swims long
distances from its
breeding areas.

*Longer upper
lobe*

TAIL OF HORN SHARK

FIN FACTS

• Sharks steer with
their body and tail; the
other fins control up-
and-down and rolling
movements of the body.

• The horny rods of
shark fins are cut off
and dried to make soup.

• The inner edge of the
male's pelvic fins forms
a pair of mating organs
called claspers.

INSIDE THE BODY

IMMEDIATELY BENEATH the skin of a shark lie the zigzag muscles that swing the body from side to side as it swin In the body cavity below is the heart and digestive system. The intestine is fairly straight, apart from a special scroll- or spiral-shaped valve that adds to the area in which digested food can be absorbed. Contrary to popular belief, sharks are not stupid – they have a larger brain for their body size than most bony fish.

Dorsal fin

Segmented swimming muscles

Spiral valve

Rectal gland

First dorsal fin

Pancreas

Spleen, produces red blood cells

BODY FACTS

• Large olfactory lobes in the brain show how important the sense of smell is to a shark.

• The tongue is supported by a pad of cartilage.

• The gallbladder releases a greenish fluid called bile into the gut; it aids digestion.

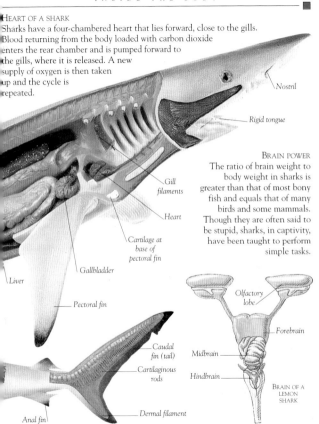

HEART OF A SHARK
Sharks have a four-chambered heart that lies forward, close to the gills.
Blood returning from the body loaded with carbon dioxide
enters the rear chamber and is pumped forward to
the gills, where it is released. A new
supply of oxygen is then taken
up and the cycle is
repeated.

Nostril

Rigid tongue

Gill
filaments

Heart

Cartilage at
base of
pectoral fin

Gallbladder

Liver

Pectoral fin

Caudal
fin (tail)

Cartilaginous
rods

Anal fin

Dermal filament

BRAIN POWER
The ratio of brain weight to
body weight in sharks is
greater than that of most bony
fish and equals that of many
birds and some mammals.
Though they are often said to
be stupid, sharks, in captivity,
have been taught to perform
simple tasks.

Olfactory
lobe

Forebrain

Midbrain

Hindbrain

BRAIN OF A
LEMON
SHARK

Gills and liver

A shark breathes by taking water into its mouth and pumping it over the gills that lie behind its head. As the water flows past, oxygen in it is removed and passes into the bloodstream to be used in the shark's body. The liver contains high quantities of oil that aid buoyancy – like the swim bladder of a bony fish.

GILLS

SHUT
As the shark takes water into its mouth (the equivalent of breathing in), the gill slits are closed.

OPEN
Water and carbon dioxide waste are expelled when the gill slits are open.

EATING AND BREATHING
Basking sharks use their gill slits for feeding as well as breathing. Attached to the gill supports are comblike structures called gill rakers that filter plankton from seawater.

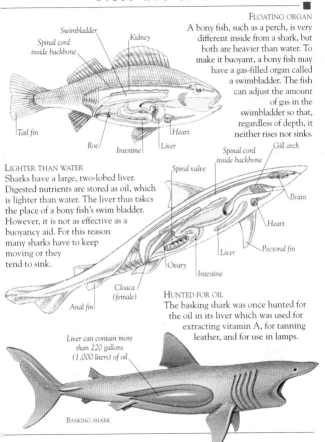

FLOATING ORGAN

A bony fish, such as a perch, is very different inside from a shark, but both are heavier than water. To make it buoyant, a bony fish may have a gas-filled organ called a swimbladder. The fish can adjust the amount of gas in the swimbladder so that, regardless of depth, it neither rises nor sinks.

Swimbladder

Spinal cord inside backbone

Kidney

Tail fin

Roe

Intestine

Heart

Liver

LIGHTER THAN WATER

Sharks have a large, two-lobed liver. Digested nutrients are stored as oil, which is lighter than water. The liver thus takes the place of a bony fish's swim bladder. However, it is not as effective as a buoyancy aid. For this reason many sharks have to keep moving or they tend to sink.

Spiral valve

Spinal cord inside backbone

Gill arch

Brain

Heart

Liver

Pectoral fin

Ovary

Intestine

Cloaca (female)

Anal fin

HUNTED FOR OIL

The basking shark was once hunted for the oil in its liver which was used for extracting vitamin A, for tanning leather, and for use in lamps.

Liver can contain more than 220 gallons (1,000 liters) of oil

BASKING SHARK

JAWS AND TEETH

SHARKS HAVE UPPER AND LOWER jaws, but, unlike most other animals with backbones, their jaws are only loosely attached to the skull. When a shark bites its prey, the jaws are forced forward, allowing the teeth to be used more efficiently.

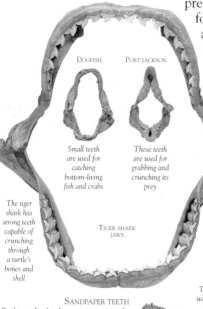

DOGFISH

PORT JACKSON

Living sharks cannot open their jaws as wide as this

Small teeth are used for catching bottom-living fish and crabs

These teeth are used for grabbing and crunching its prey

The tiger shark has strong teeth capable of crunching through a turtle's bones and shell

TIGER SHARK JAWS

RENEWABLE TEETH
Shark teeth are arranged in rows. There are usually six or more rows of replacement teeth constantly developing in the mouth. The teeth in the front row slash at prey. As soon as one becomes slightly blunted or damaged, it falls out and another tooth from behind slips into place.

Tiny teeth not used for feeding

SANDPAPER TEETH
Basking sharks do not tear or crush their food, so their teeth are small, resembling coarse sandpaper.

CRUSHING TEETH

Port Jackson sharks feed on hard-shelled animals without backbones, such as crabs and sea urchins. A pad of small, sharp teeth in the front of their mouths seizes the prey from the seabed. In the back of the jaws is a battery of flat, pebblelike teeth that crushes the armor of their victims.

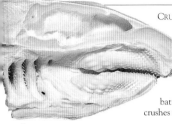

SECTION THROUGH A PORT JACKSON'S JAWS

BITE-SIZE HOLES

The cookiecutter shark is named after the circular chunks of flesh it bites from its prey. It has small, sharp teeth and feeds on big fish, whales, and seals, all much larger than itself. Cookiecutters shed an entire row of teeth at one time, usually swallowing them with their food.

Cookiecutter's lips cling onto prey like suckers

HUNGRY TEETH

The sand tiger raises its overhanging snout as it attacks its prey. Its pointed teeth are ideal for grabbing and holding fish. It has a huge appetite and may eat more than 99 lb (45 kg) of food in a single meal.

SKELETONS

SHARKS ARE DIFFERENT from all other animals and humans in that their skeletons contain no bone. Instead, they are made from a soft, flexible, gristly material called cartilage. In some sharks, part of the skeleton is strengthened with calcium salts, particularly in the bones of the back, jaws, and braincase.

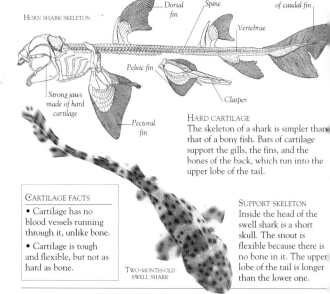

HORN SHARK SKELETON

Dorsal fin

Spine

Longer upper lobe of caudal fin

Vertebrae

Pelvic fin

Strong jaws made of hard cartilage

Clasper

Pectoral fin

TWO-MONTH-OLD SWELL SHARK

HARD CARTILAGE
The skeleton of a shark is simpler than that of a bony fish. Bars of cartilage support the gills, the fins, and the bones of the back, which run into the upper lobe of the tail.

CARTILAGE FACTS
• Cartilage has no blood vessels running through it, unlike bone.

• Cartilage is tough and flexible, but not as hard as bone.

SUPPORT SKELETON
Inside the head of the swell shark is a short skull. The snout is flexible because there is no bone in it. The upper lobe of the tail is longer than the lower one.

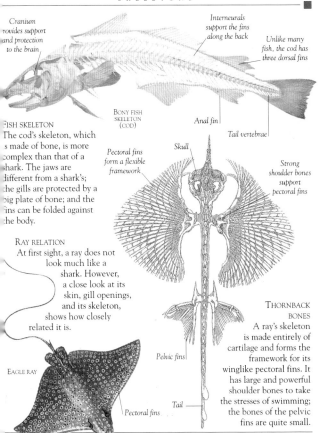

Cranium provides support and protection to the brain

Interneurals support the fins along the back

Unlike many fish, the cod has three dorsal fins

BONY FISH SKELETON (COD)

Anal fin

Tail vertebrae

FISH SKELETON
The cod's skeleton, which is made of bone, is more complex than that of a shark. The jaws are different from a shark's; the gills are protected by a big plate of bone; and the fins can be folded against the body.

Pectoral fins form a flexible framework

Skull

Strong shoulder bones support pectoral fins

RAY RELATION
At first sight, a ray does not look much like a shark. However, a close look at its skin, gill openings, and its skeleton, shows how closely related it is.

EAGLE RAY

Pelvic fins

Tail

Pectoral fins

THORNBACK BONES
A ray's skeleton is made entirely of cartilage and forms the framework for its winglike pectoral fins. It has large and powerful shoulder bones to take the stresses of swimming; the bones of the pelvic fins are quite small.

SKIN

A SHARK'S SKIN is protected, not by scales, but
by small, hard "skin teeth" or dermal denticles.
Denticles vary in shape from one part of the
body to another. They are rounded on its
snout and pointed on its back; in the jaws,
the denticles develop into powerful teeth.

*19th-century
samurai sword*

DENTICLES
X 10 MAGNIFICATION

SKIN TEETH
A shark's dermal denticles
are covered with enamel.
Below the enamel is a layer
of dentine, which is the
basic material of most
teeth. Each dentine
layer has a cavity
which has a bony base,
containing blood
vessels and nerves, set
deep in the skin.

HARDWEARING
DECORATION
The skin of many sharks
is used for making leather
or a natural type of
sandpaper called
shagreen. This Japanese
samurai sword is
enclosed in a sheath of
ray skin. The skin has
been polished and
lacquered so that its
denticles are smooth.

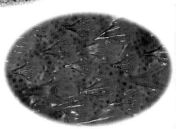

SKIN DETAIL OF LESSER SPOTTED DOGFISH

It is possible to see growth rings on the scale of a fish which indicate its age

FISH SCALE

BRAMBLE SHARK SKIN
A few kinds of shark have very small denticles or even smooth skin. A bramble shark has scattered denticles, some of which have a tuft of little spikes like the thorns of a blackberry.

As the shark grows, the denticles are shed and replaced by larger ones

SCALE BONES
The scales of a bony fish, such as a salmon or perch, are made of thin slips of bone, set in the skin like the overlapping tiles on a roof. As the fish grows, the scales increase in size.

WELL DISGUISED
The wobbegong matches the color of the seabed on which it lies. Its prey is lured by the fringe of tassels around its mouth. The wobbegong's mouth looks like seaweed to the creatures it eats.

LIVING AND SURVIVING

SENSES

A SHARK'S SENSES tell it about the world in which it lives. Besides being able to see, smell, and hear, a shark can also sense movements and electrical fields made by other animals in the water. Using this sense of "touch," it locates food or enemies. The sharpness of a shark's senses varies from one species to another depending on lifestyle.

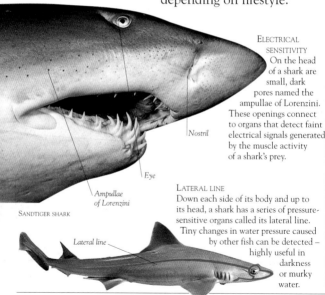

ELECTRICAL SENSITIVITY
On the head of a shark are small, dark pores named the ampullae of Lorenzini. These openings connect to organs that detect faint electrical signals generated by the muscle activity of a shark's prey.

Nostril

Eye

Ampullae of Lorenzini

SANDTIGER SHARK

LATERAL LINE
Down each side of its body and up to its head, a shark has a series of pressure-sensitive organs called its lateral line. Tiny changes in water pressure caused by other fish can be detected – highly useful in darkness or murky water.

Lateral line

BALANCE MECHANISM

When a shark turns or changes level, liquid moves against the hairlike organs that line the canals of the ear. Ear stones move as the shark changes speed, keeping it informed of position and movement.

Large nostrils of epaulette shark

SCENT DETECTORS

As a shark swims, water constantly flows into its nostril sacs, which are lined with scent-detecting cells.

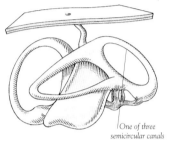

One of three semicircular canals

EYES

Sharks can see well in dim light. Their eyes have a layer of cells called a tapetum that reflects light back onto the retina. In bright light they can close the pupil to a narrow slit. Some sharks have a light-blocking screen to filter light.

DOGFISH WITH CLOSED PUPIL

HORN SHARK'S PUPIL

RAY EYE WITH SCREEN

Barbels

FOOD FEELERS

Nurse sharks feed mostly on animals without backbones. Fleshy, finger-like barbels at the front of the mouth probe the sand of the seabed for food, perhaps also gathering information about the smell and taste of the prey.

FEEDING HABITS

SHARKS EAT MANY different types of food, but all are flesh-eaters. Most eat small fish or invertebrates and some will grab carrion when they can. Three large species filter food, known as plankton, from the sea. Some sharks hunt large animals, including sea lions and other sharks.

GENTLE EATER
The whale shark mainly feeds on plankton. Meshlike filters sift tiny creatures from the water that passes over its gills. On occasion the whale shark becomes an active hunter, preying on shoals of small fish, such as anchovy.

FEEDING FACTS
• Sharks do not need to feed every day.
• Undigested food may remain in the stomach for several days.
• Smell and the lateral line are the principal senses used by the shark to lead it to food.

SHARP TEETH
The horn shark uses its sense of smell to locate animals such as sea urchins and shellfish on which it feeds. They are caught with its sharp front teeth and crushed with flat teeth in the back of its mouth.

Downward-directed nostrils

This shark grows to about 3 ft (1 m)

NIGHT FEEDER
The lesser spotted dogfish lives near land in water up to 100 m (328 ft) deep. During the day it hides among seaweed. At night it searches for shellfish and small fish.

TEETH

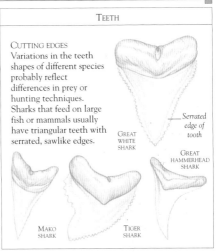

CUTTING EDGES
Variations in the teeth shapes of different species probably reflect differences in prey or hunting techniques. Sharks that feed on large fish or mammals usually have triangular teeth with serrated, sawlike edges.

GREAT WHITE SHARK

Serrated edge of tooth

GREAT HAMMERHEAD SHARK

MAKO SHARK

TIGER SHARK

SWIFT HUNTERS
Unlike its relatives, the tiger shark will try eating virtually anything at least once. It grows up to 18ft (5.5m), with a very wide mouth, powerful jaws, and the sharpest of bites. There are few marine creatures that the tiger shark cannot tackle.

Snout turns up as shark attacks

TIGER SHARK WITH PREY

MATING AND FERTILIZATION

WHEN SOME MALE AND FEMALE sharks meet, the male chases and bites the female, encouraging her to mate. Sharks' mating behavior ensures that, unlike bony fish, the eggs are fertilized inside the female. In some species, the female lays eggs; in others, the young develop inside their mother – while some sharks are capable of both.

Males are usually smaller than their mates

MATING
Small male sharks, such as dogfish mate by winding their flexible body around the female. Some larger sharks mate side to side. Females often have thicker skin than the males' teeth to prevent injury during courtship.

REPRODUCTIVE ORGANS
Male sharks have a pair of claspers that are formed from part of the pelvic fins. During mating one of them is inserted into the female opening, called the cloaca. Sperm is released into the female to fertilize the eggs.

Cloaca

Clasper

FEMALE PELVIC FINS

MALE PELVIC FINS

EGG CASES

Shark eggs have a large egg yolk that is protected in a horny or leathery case. Female horn sharks lay spiral egg cases which they wedge into clefts in rocks for safety from other creatures.

SPIRAL EGG CASE
OF HORN SHARK

*Embryo
dogfish inside
an egg case*

EMBRYO DEVELOPMENT

Sharks take up to a year to develop. When a pup hatches, it is at least 4 in (10 cm) long. As a result, it stands a better chance of survival than one of the many tiny young produced by most bony fish.

*The embryo
is nourished
with a large
yolk sac*

HIDING PLACE

Most dogfish lay their eggs in dense beds of seaweed. The curly, ribbonlike ends on the corners of the egg cases tangle with seaweed fronds and are held safely. The movement of the water brings oxygen to the developing embryo.

DEVELOPMENT OF YOUNG

IN SOME SHARKS, the female produces thin-shelled
eggs, which remain inside her body until they hatch.
Sometimes baby sharks hatch at an early stage, but do
not leave their mother's body. Each one continues to
grow, feeding on its egg's large yolk sac.

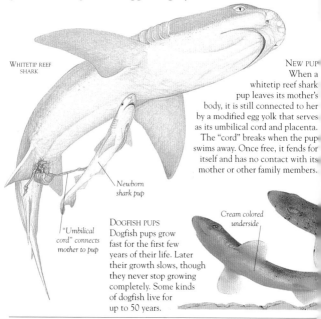

WHITETIP REEF
SHARK

NEW PUP
When a
whitetip reef shark
pup leaves its mother's
body, it is still connected to her
by a modified egg yolk that serves
as its umbilical cord and placenta.
The "cord" breaks when the pup
swims away. Once free, it fends for
itself and has no contact with its
mother or other family members.

*Newborn
shark pup*

Cream colored
underside

*"Umbilical
cord" connects
mother to pup*

DOGFISH PUPS
Dogfish pups grow
fast for the first few
years of their life. Later
their growth slows, though
they never stop growing
completely. Some kinds
of dogfish live for
up to 50 years.

BIRTH FOR SURVIVAL

Birth is usually a rapid process to protect the newborn pup from enemies waiting to take advantage of a female or young in difficulty. Remoras are often nearby, waiting for the afterbirth, which they eat quickly. This reduces the likelihood of predators – including other sharks – being attracted to the birth scene.

TAIL FIRST
As a precaution against complications during birth, sharks are born tail first. The pup stands a better chance of survival if its head is still protected by its mother's body.

ENDANGERED NEWBORN
Game fishermen deliberately pursue female sharks since they are generally larger than males. Sometimes the trauma of being caught results in the female giving birth early to a litter of pups.

Pair of dogfish pups 10 days old and 4 in (10 cm) long

Soon the pups will feed on small creatures, such as shrimps

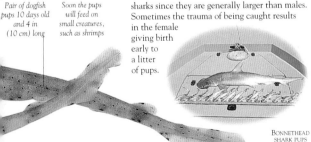

BONNETHEAD
SHARK PUPS

THE BODY CLOCK

ALL ANIMALS LIVE to rhythms dictated by the sun and the seasons. These are translated into patterns of behavior such as sleeping, breeding, and migrating. Even the lives of deep-sea sharks are regulated by their body clocks.

The greenland shark is a deep-water "sleeper"

SLEEPER SHARK

The Greenland shark and its close relatives are often known as "sleeper sharks" because as well as being having a generally inactive lifestyle, they spend a lot of time resting motionless on the seabed, apparently asleep.

SLEEPING FACTS

• Dreaming has been observed in bony fish, but not yet in sharks.

• Some sharks must keep swimming in order to breathe, so they have to sleep on the move, dozing as they travel.

WINTER DOZE

It used to be thought that basking sharks hibernated during the winter because we do not see them. Satellite tracking has now shown that they remain active, but live much deeper than normal, well out of our sight.

FAST ASLEEP

Nurse sharks are among several kinds of reef sharks known to rest for long periods on the seafloor. They appear to be breathing slowly, but if disturbed will swim off in a flurry as though awakened from a deep sleep.

BLUE SHARK

Blue sharks do not sleep on the seabed

MIGRATION RHYTHM

Blue sharks migrate each year, moving between breeding and feeding grounds at definite times of the year. Like other oceanic sharks, blue sharks may rest without sinking to the bottom.

GREATEST TRAVELER

Tagging, mainly in the US, has shown that some blue sharks cover more than 3,726 miles (6,000 km) a year. More work remains to be done before the movements of different populations can be fully understood.

RELEASE OF BLUE SHARKS

TAGGING RELEASE AREAS OFF US COAST

TAGGING RELEASE AREAS ELSEWHERE

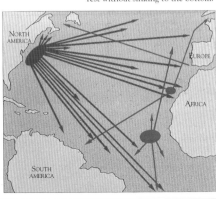

NORTH AMERICA

EUROPE

AFRICA

SOUTH AMERICA

FRIENDS AND FOES

SHARKS HAVE FEW natural enemies,
but many creatures known as
commensals live close to, or are
attached to, large sharks. Some of
these creatures are able to live
without the shark, unlike parasites
such as tapeworms, that cannot
survive away from their host's body.

Tentacle

Head

Suction pad

REMORAS
Remoras are sometimes
called "shark suckers" because they
attach themselves to a shark with a ridged sucker on top
of their heads. They may feed on the shark's food scraps
and are thought to aid the shark by also feeding on tiny
parasites lodged in its skin.

TAPEWORM
Inside the
gut of a
shark live
hundreds of parasites
called tapeworms.
They feed on digested
food and can grow up
to 1 ft (30 cm) long.

PILOT FISH
In tropical
waters, agile
pilot fish swim below
sharks. They do not, as
their name suggests, guide
the shark, but benefit
from the protection
gained by traveling
with large sharks.

SHARK PARASITES

SKIN FEEDERS

Copepods are small relatives of crabs and form part of the plankton of the sea. Some become parasites on a shark's skin or gills, attaching themselves with adhesive pads and feeding on skin secretions.

FEMALE COPEPOD

MALE COPEPOD

EYE SPY

This crustacean is a parasite that feeds on the surface of the eyes of Greenland sharks. It may damage its host's vision, but by producing light it may also attract small fish for the shark to eat.

Egg sac contains thousands of eggs

EYE SPY

SHARP CLAWS

This copepod hangs on to the shark's skin, feeding partly on blood. Basking sharks are thought to rid themselves of the irritation by leaping out of the sea.

Abdomen

Soft shell

HANGERS ON

Many large oceanic animals carry barnacles. The rootlets on the fleshy stalk of the barnacle feeds on body fluids.

BARNACLE

DOLPHIN VERSUS SHARK

It is thought that dolphins drive sharks away, but this is not necessarily true. However, the bottlenose dolphin has been trained by scientists in Florida to chase and attack sharks. During these experiments, the dolphin appeared able to distinguish one shark species from another.

When sharks and dolphins share an aquarium, they usually ignore each other

BOTTLENOSE DOLPHIN

SHARKS AND HUMANS

FEAR AND LOATHING

THE SHARK IS A POWERFUL symbol of terror, and sharks
have traditionally been regarded as fearsome sea beasts
to be hunted and killed
without mercy. Sailors
once believed that
sharks preferred human
flesh to all other and,
even today, many
regard all sharks as
potential man-eaters.

HOLLYWOOD PARANOIA
The 1975 film *Jaws*, about a "killer"
great white shark, scared audiences
out of the water, and fueled
worldwide hatred and fear of sharks.
However, Peter Benchley, the author
of the novel *Jaws*, now supports
shark conservation.

ARTIST'S IMPRESSION
This engraving of a shark
cast onto a beach in
France was created more
than 100 years ago. The
mixture of features in
the illustration – size of
a great white, tail shape
of a thresher – suggests
that the artist was working
from a description, not life.

FEEDING FRENZY
This shipwreck was the front cover of a Paris magazine in 1906. It illustrated one of sailors' most common fears – that of sharks in a feeding frenzy, swarming around a sinking ship, picking off survivors one by one.

SANTA MARIA

Columbus sailed this ship

BAD OMEN
Disease was common among early explorers, and dead bodies were often thrown overboard, which sometimes attracted sharks. Superstitious sailors believed that the presence of sharks foretold further deaths.

SHIPWRECK CASUALTIES CAUSED BY SHARKS

Tragedies at sea are a rare occurence, but are made much worse by sharks. During World War II, many lives were lost when sharks closed in on wounded and struggling sailors.

SHIP	DATE	PASSENGERS AND CREW	NUMBER LOST
Valerian	1926	104	84
Principessa Mafalda	1927	1,259	314
Cape San Juan	1943	1,429	981
Indianapolis	1945	1,199	883
Ganges Ferry Boat	1975	190	50+

SUPERSTITION FACTS
• Sailors falsely believed that sharks preferred the taste of people of their own nationality.

• Sailors used to take revenge on any shark they caught by torturing it to death.

SHARK ATTACK

OF NEARLY 400 SHARK SPECIES, only ten are known to regularly attack people; most sharks are not dangerous and ignore humans unless provoked. Experts are unable to agree on the number of deaths caused by sharks.

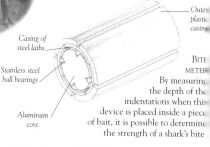

Outer plastic casing

Casing of steel laths

Stainless steel ball bearings

Aluminum core

SHALLOW WATER
Attacks on humans often take place close to the shore in shallow water. This is probably because the majority of people are found swimming and paddling in this area.

BITE METER
By measuring the depth of the indentations when this device is placed inside a piece of bait, it is possible to determine the strength of a shark's bite.

SEAL FROM BELOW

SURFER

MISTAKEN IDENTITY
Great whites mistake the silhouettes of surfers for seals as they attack from below at great speed, trying to surprise their prey. Other sharks may attack humans by mistake if the water is cloudy, or if people unknowingly swim among the sharks' fish prey at night.

PUBLIC ENEMY
The tiger shark is large and powerful enough to attack most sea creatures. Its diet includes seals, dolphins, sea snakes, hammerhead sharks, and turtles. Many humans have been killed by this shark.

RIVER MENACE
Bull sharks are dreaded in many parts of the tropics because they venture up rivers, posing a real threat to wildlife and humans alike.

GREAT HUNTER
The great white is deservedly the most feared shark of all. It can swim fast enough to jump right out of the water and is large enough to attack any animal in the sea. It has even been known to attack and sink small boats.

Fatalities

A person is more likely to be struck by lightning than attacked by a shark. Although experts disagree, it has been suggested that since 1940 there have been an average of only 28 attacks each year, one-third of which were fatal, worldwide. These figures include attacks made by sharks in self-defense or by those that were caught or harrassed in some way.

GREENLAND

NORTH AMERICA

ATLANTIC OCEAN

There are many recorded attacks in the West Indies

SOUTH AMERICA

PACIFIC OCEAN

Few attacks recorded in this area

ATTACK GEOGRAPHY
Almost all shark attacks take place in warm seas because a greater variety of sharks are found there alongside a greater number of swimmers. On the map opposite, shark attacks are indicated in orange. Where the color is darker there is a higher incidence of attack in that area.

AGGRESSIVE BODY LANGUAGE

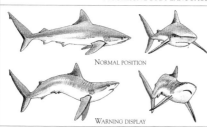

NORMAL POSITION

WARNING DISPLAY

Some sharks attack without warning, but the gray reef shark warns intruders. It displays a threatening posture by raising its snout and lowering its pectoral fins. If a diver does not retreat, the shark will attack.

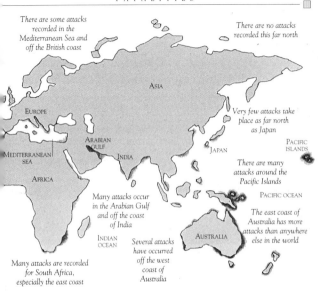

There are some attacks recorded in the Mediterranean Sea and off the British coast

There are no attacks recorded this far north

ASIA

EUROPE

Very few attacks take place as far north as Japan

ARABIAN GULF

MEDITERRANEAN SEA

INDIA

JAPAN

PACIFIC ISLANDS

AFRICA

There are many attacks around the Pacific Islands

PACIFIC OCEAN

Many attacks occur in the Arabian Gulf and off the coast of India

INDIAN OCEAN

Several attacks have occurred off the west coast of Australia

AUSTRALIA

The east coast of Australia has more attacks than anywhere else in the world

Many attacks are recorded for South Africa, especially the east coast

FATAL ATTACKS

More people now survive attacks by sharks because of faster and better medical attention. These statistics are from an Australian analysis of fatalities in shallow seas.

Each year an average of 92 percent of deaths are due to drowning...

...about 8 percent are killed scuba diving

...and less than 1 percent dies from shark attack

SOUND ADVICE

• Do not swim at dusk or after dark when sharks may be feeding.

• Beware if there are unusually large numbers of fish nearby.

• Bait from fishing boats may attract sharks.

DEFENSE

ALL KINDS OF DEVICES – nets, repellents, electrical barriers, air bubbles – have been specially designed to protect swimmers and divers from the dangers of shark attack. Few, if any, have proved entirely successful, and some have proved dangerous to other sea creatures.

SHARK NET
Popular swimming beaches are often secured against sharks with mesh nets. Nets are costly and need constant maintenance, and unfortunately also trap many harmless creatures such as turtles, rays, and dolphins.

ARMOR SUIT
Some divers at risk from large, active sharks wear protective suits made of steel mesh, like medieval chain-mail armor. The suit prevents a shark's teeth from penetrating the diver's body, though there may be severe bruising from the shark's jaws.

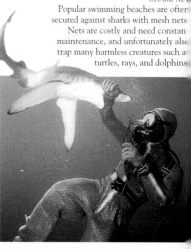

DETAIL OF SHARK SUIT WITH TOOTH
OF GREAT WHITE

CAGE PROTECTION

Some of the most dramatic pictures of sharks have been shot by underwater filmmakers enclosed by thick, metal cages. A shark's ability to detect underwater electric fields has possibly been the cause of numerous attacks on cages.

A bangstick can be effective in experienced hands

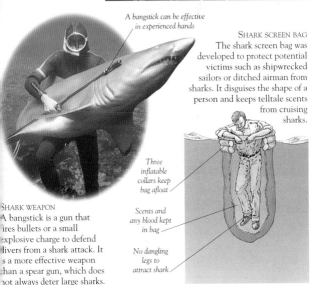

SHARK SCREEN BAG

The shark screen bag was developed to protect potential victims such as shipwrecked sailors or ditched airman from sharks. It disguises the shape of a person and keeps telltale scents from cruising sharks.

Three inflatable collars keep bag afloat

Scents and any blood kept in bag

No dangling legs to attract shark

SHARK WEAPON

A bangstick is a gun that fires bullets or a small explosive charge to defend divers from a shark attack. It is a more effective weapon than a spear gun, which does not always deter large sharks.

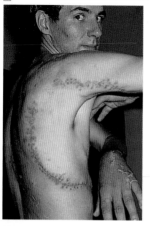

SURVIVORS

SHARK ATTACKS are not universally fatal. Most survivors have been physically fit and have remained calm during the attack. They have also been swimming near friends or within reach of a boat. Some people have survived by fighting back – attacking the shark's eyes with their bare hands.

MIRACULOUS RECOVERY

Australian diver Rodney Fox was taking part in a spear-fishing competition near Adelaide in 1963 when he was attacked by a great white shark. His upper body was badly crushed and torn. He was rushed to the hospital, where he received 462 stitches in a 4-hour operation.

Surfers lying on their boards are an easy target

SURVIVAL FACTS

- Most sharks will only strike once.
- Blood loss and shock are the most dangerous effects of shark bites.
- About one-quarter of all attacks kill the victim.

LUCKY ESCAPE

Surfers can be at risk from sharks, athough few are attacked. This surfer's board was bitten by a 10–13 ft (3–4 m) shark near a coral reef in Hawaii.

SIR BROOKS WATSON
One of the most famous survivors of a shark attack was Brooks Watson, who lost a leg to a shark in 1749. He later became Lord Mayor of London and was knighted.

Neptune, Roman god of the sea

COAT OF ARMS
Sir Brooks Watson recalled his history on this coat of arms. In the top left of the shield is his severed leg.

The motto means "Under God's shield"

FORGIVING DIVER
Henri Bource lost a leg off the coast of Australia, where he was attacked by a great white in 1964. He still dives and does not blame the shark for its behavior.

CLOSE CALL
Valerie Taylor is a shark expert who has watched and filmed sharks for many years. In the photograph above she has been bitten on the leg. She was not seriously injured but still needed hospital treatment.

FOLKLORE

THE INHABITANTS of some Pacific Islands regard certain sharks as gods, or spirits of their ancestors. Ancient Polynesians often believed that sharks were spirits sent by sorcerers to bring death and ill fortune. In some parts of West Africa, the shark is sacred and if one is accidentally killed, sacrificial rites must be performed.

SHARK/
BONITO
This charm, from Ulawa in the Solomon Islands, is of a bonito fish on one side and a shark on the other. Hunters carried carvings like these in their canoes, hoping to attract the bonito and repel large sharks.

The bonito hunting ritual was an annual event

Carving made of wood, inlaid with pearl

LATE-19TH-CENTURY SHARK CHARM

Sharklike head

FOLKLORE FACTS
• Some Pacific Islanders believed that sharks would protect and save them from drowning.
• In Borneo, to stop babies from crying, the saw from a sawfish is covered in cloth and hung over the cradle.

SEA SPIRIT
Solomon Islanders believed that when people died their ghosts inhabited the bodies of sharks. This sea spirit has a head with fins like a shark. It was probably used to protect its maker from danger when fishing at sea.

64

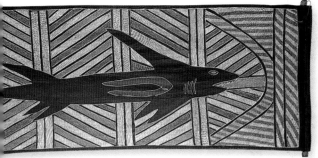

BARK PAINTING

This painting of a shark by the Yirrakala people of the Northern Territory, Australia, shows the huge two-lobed liver. Sharks were important to many native people as a source of food and oil.

Early-20th-century rattle from Papua New Guinea for attracting sharks

SHARK MASK

Native Americans from Alaska carve animal masks for use on ceremonial occasions. This mask is of a ground shark with a frog in its mouth. It is made of painted wood and leather, inlaid with abalone shell.

Rattle made from coconut shells

RATTLES

Some Pacific Islanders hunt sharks as a test of strength and manhood; others use the shark skin and teeth for decoration and weapons. The shark is lured using underwater rattles.

SHARK DIRECTORY

MACKEREL SHARKS

THE GREAT WHITE, the porbeagle, and the mako are collectively known as mackerel sharks. The name not only refers to the type of fast-swimming fish that they eat, but also to these sharks' mackerel-like, streamlined bodies. As with many shark groups, little is known about their breeding behavior or migratory habits.

GREAT WHITE

WARM-BLOODED
Porbeagle sharks prefer more temperate seas and may be seen near the British and North American coasts in summer. They are heavily built and partly warm-blooded, being able to keep their body temperature several degrees higher than their surroundings.

MACKEREL FACTS
• Mackerel sharks make spectacular leaps when hooked by game fishermen.

• Unborn makos and porbeagles survive in the uterus by eating the unfertilized eggs.

• Normally only two pups are born at a time.

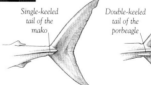

Single-keeled tail of the mako

Double-keeled tail of the porbeagle

TAIL FINS
The tail lobes of mackerel sharks are nearly equal in size. Mako and porbeagles have small stabilizing keels at the base of their tail. The keel probably helps the fish to stay on course when making tight turns.

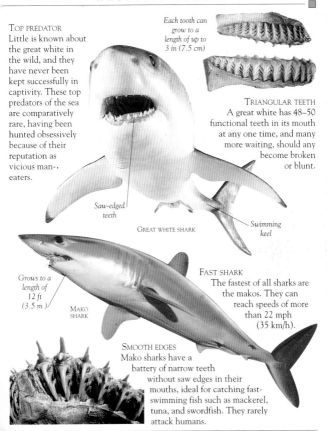

TOP PREDATOR
Little is known about the great white in the wild, and they have never been kept successfully in captivity. These top predators of the sea are comparatively rare, having been hunted obsessively because of their reputation as vicious man-eaters.

Each tooth can grow to a length of up to 3 in (7.5 cm)

TRIANGULAR TEETH
A great white has 48–50 functional teeth in its mouth at any one time, and many more waiting, should any become broken or blunt.

Saw-edged teeth

GREAT WHITE SHARK

Swimming keel

Grows to a length of 12 ft (3.5 m)

MAKO SHARK

FAST SHARK
The fastest of all sharks are the makos. They can reach speeds of more than 22 mph (35 km/h).

SMOOTH EDGES
Mako sharks have a battery of narrow teeth without saw edges in their mouths, ideal for catching fast-swimming fish such as mackerel, tuna, and swordfish. They rarely attack humans.

HAMMERS AND THRESHERS

THE HAMMERHEAD and the thresher shark are not closely related, but both are easy to recognize: one for its extraordinary head; the other for its long tail, which may make up half its length. The teeth of close relatives of hammerheads and thresher sharks have been found in rocks at least 60 million years old.

LONG TAIL
Most threshers are surface swimmers, hunting small fish such as herring or sardines. Thresher pups may be 5 ft (1.5 m) long at birth. One species has very large eyes and lives in deep water.

Upper lobe of tail may be half the size of body

Can grow up to 20 ft (6 m) long

Threshers weigh about 1,000 lb (450 kg)

THRESHER SHARK

BONNETHEAD
The shovel-shaped head, with eyes and nostrils on the outer edge, marks the bonnethead shark as a small relative of the great hammerheads. It often comes into shallow bays to hunt small fish, crabs, and shrimps. Like all hammerheads, it produces live young.

BONNETHEAD SHARK

Gill slits

Mouth is located under the head

SENSORY HEAD
Hammerheads swing their heads from side to side as they swim, testing the water for the presence of stingrays, their main prey. Sometimes the sting of a ray will become embedded in a shark's jaws, causing its teeth to grow abnormally.

HAMMERHEAD SHARK

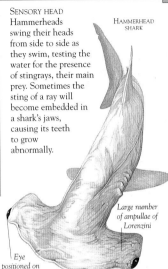

Large number of ampullae of Lorenzini

Eye positioned on side of head

HAMMER SCHOOLS
Most hammerheads are solitary hunters, but scalloped hammerheads will school by the hundred. The adults patrol around the edges of the school, while the pups gather in the center for protection.

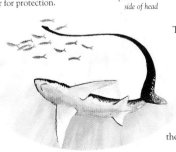

LETHAL TAIL
Thresher sharks are thought to work in pairs, lashing their tails to frighten groups of fish into a tight pack that can be caught easily. Threshers are sought after by game fishermen, as they are exciting prey. However, they can inflict severe injuries with their powerful tails.

REQUIEM SHARKS

SAILORS IN DAYS GONE BY did not name this group of sharks because of any connection with death. They called them requiem, or "rest," sharks because they were often seen in fair weather. Some requiems live in the open ocean, while others, such as those shown here, are found close to the shore.

WARNING SIGNAL

Divers may encounter gray reef sharks since they are often found in lagoons and on the outer edges of reefs. They are not usually dangerous, but may be territorial. If it feels threatened, a gray reef shark will warn intruders by arching its back into an aggressive posture.

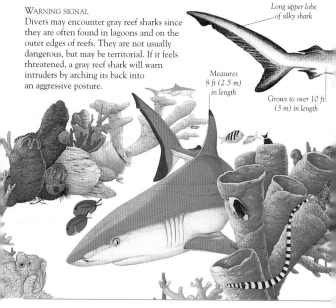

Long upper lobe of silky shark

Measures 8 ft (2.5 m) in length

Grows to over 10 ft (3 m) in length

LAGOON DWELLER
The lemon shark is often found in shallow lagoons. It eats crabs, octopuses, and seabirds. It also eats stingrays, and often has stings embedded in its mouth as a result. It is born in shallow water where it stays for some years before gradually venturing out into open seas.

LEMON SHARK

SILKY SHARK

SILKY SMOOTH
Named because of its small and smooth dermal denticles, the silky shark's sides do not have the rough feel of those of most other sharks. It is one of the most common species of shark, often taking tuna from the nets of fishermen.

Dorsal fin sticks out of the water in shallows

Body length can reach 6 ft (1.8 m)

Denticles of silky shark are only 0.01 in (0.25 mm) across

AGGRESSIVE SPECIES
Often lying in reef pools only 2 ft (60 cm) deep, blacktip reef sharks are not to be trifled with. These keen hunters have been known to nip the ankles of unwary human waders by mistake.

REQUIEM FACTS
• Females store their mate's sperm until the next year, when the eggs are fertilized.

• Requiems produce about 14 young in a litter.

• Requiem pups grow faster than other sharks.

More requiems

All requiem sharks shown here are large species that may be dangerous. The blue shark lives in almost all the oceans of the world and is responsible for some attacks on shipwrecked sailors. Tiger sharks are found only in warm seas, close to the shore. Bull sharks sometimes venture into freshwater.

BLUE SHARK

TRAVELING HUNTER
Blue sharks are the great travelers of the shark world, covering huge distances each year. They do not dive deeply for food, but hunt almost any kind of surface-living fish. They particularly like whale meat and are known to gather in "feeding frenzies" when they find a whale carcass.

REQUIEM FACTS

• The distinctive stripes on a tiger shark fade as the shark ages.

• Female blue sharks have skin thicker than the length of the male's teeth to prevent injury during courtship.

OCEANIC WHITETIP SHARK

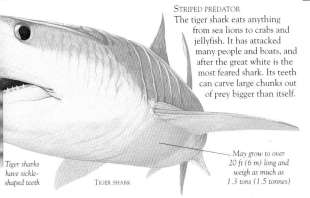

STRIPED PREDATOR
The tiger shark eats anything from sea lions to crabs and jellyfish. It has attacked many people and boats, and after the great white is the most feared shark. Its teeth can carve large chunks out of prey bigger than itself.

Tiger sharks have sickle-shaped teeth

TIGER SHARK

May grow to over 20 ft (6 m) long and weigh as much as 1.3 tons (1.5 tonnes)

MOTHER'S HELP
To protect their pups from predators of the open sea, female lemon sharks may beach themselves in the shallows of mangrove swamps to give birth. The pups gradually migrate to deeper waters as they grow.

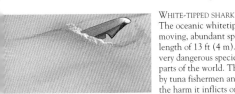

WHITE-TIPPED SHARK
The oceanic whitetip shark is a slow-moving, abundant species that grows to a length of 13 ft (4 m). It is a fearless and very dangerous species found in most parts of the world. This shark is despised by tuna fishermen and whalers because of the harm it inflicts on their catches.

REQUIEM COUSINS

MOST SHARK SPECIES do not grow much larger than
3–4 ft (1–1.2 m) long, the numerous dogfish species
being a good example. True dogfish lack the anal
fin of other sharks and live in very deep
waters. The small sharks that we do see
near the shore, such as smooth-
hound and leopard sharks, are
close cousins of the requiems.

*Grows to an
average of
4 ft (1.2 m)*

*Some species
emit an
unpleasant smell*

Sharp nose

SMOOTH-HOUND
SHARK

ON THE MENU
Because of
their size and
tender flesh,
smooth-hound
sharks are an important food
fish. They are easily caught
close to shore, and are eaten by
people all around the world.

COMMON, BUT UNDER THREAT
The spiny dogfish is perhaps the world's most
abundant shark. But its numbers have declined
drastically in many places as a result of
commercial fishing. Males and females
swim at different depths, so if a
trawler catches all the fish
at one depth, the rest
cannot breed because
they are all the same sex.

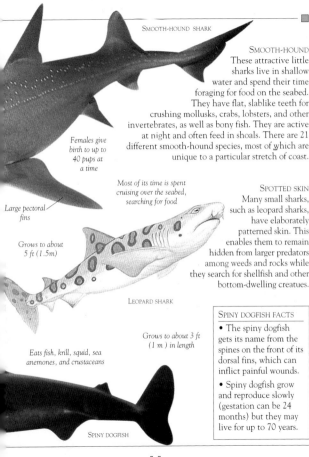

SMOOTH-HOUND SHARK

SMOOTH-HOUND

These attractive little sharks live in shallow water and spend their time foraging for food on the seabed. They have flat, slablike teeth for crushing mollusks, crabs, lobsters, and other invertebrates, as well as bony fish. They are active at night and often feed in shoals. There are 21 different smooth-hound species, most of which are unique to a particular stretch of coast.

Females give birth to up to 40 pups at a time

Most of its time is spent cruising over the seabed, searching for food

Large pectoral fins

Grows to about 5 ft (1.5m)

SPOTTED SKIN

Many small sharks, such as leopard sharks, have elaborately patterned skin. This enables them to remain hidden from larger predators among weeds and rocks while they search for shellfish and other bottom-dwelling creatures.

LEOPARD SHARK

Grows to about 3 ft (1 m) in length

Eats fish, krill, squid, sea anemones, and crustaceans

SPINY DOGFISH

SPINY DOGFISH FACTS

• The spiny dogfish gets its name from the spines on the front of its dorsal fins, which can inflict painful wounds.

• Spiny dogfish grow and reproduce slowly (gestation can be 24 months) but they may live for up to 70 years.

CARPET AND NURSE SHARKS

MOST KINDS OF CARPET and nurse sharks live in Australia and east Asian waters. They live on the seabed, and all are sluggish swimmers. Most are small, with sharp teeth for eating small fish and invertebrates. Nurse sharks were named by early explorers after an ancient word meaning "big fish."

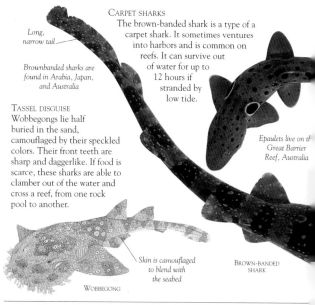

CARPET SHARKS
The brown-banded shark is a type of a carpet shark. It sometimes ventures into harbors and is common on reefs. It can survive out of water for up to 12 hours if stranded by low tide.

Long, narrow tail

Brownbanded sharks are found in Arabia, Japan, and Australia

TASSEL DISGUISE
Wobbegongs lie half buried in the sand, camouflaged by their speckled colors. Their front teeth are sharp and daggerlike. If food is scarce, these sharks are able to clamber out of the water and cross a reef, from one rock pool to another.

Epaulets live on the Great Barrier Reef, Australia

Skin is camouflaged to blend with the seabed

BROWN-BANDED SHARK

WOBBEGONG

NURSE SHARK
Nurse sharks hunt at night using their barbels to search for small fish. They cope well in aquariums and some have been known to survive in captivity for up to 25 years.

Barbels used for finding food

Nurse sharks can sometimes be seen in reef pools, resting in groups.

Stripes make it difficult to see shark in shallow water

Stripes become less vivid as the shark ages

ZEBRA SHARK
The zebra shark is named after the stripes that break up its shape as it lies in shallow water. It grows up to 10 ft (3 m) long; its tail accounts for half its length.

EPAULET SHARK
This shark is common and harmless to humans. It searches for food in shallow pools. Like the wobbegong it can "walk" from pool to pool, using its pectoral fins to haul itself along.

EPAULET SHARK

NOT A REAL NURSE
Although the sandtiger shark is known as the gray nurse shark in Australia, it is far more active than the nurse sharks. Usually not aggressive unless provoked, its distinctive, ragged teeth can cause serious injury.

CATSHARKS

ONE-THIRD of all sharks belong to the catshark family.
Small, slender fish, with two dorsal fins set well back
on the body, most are found in deep water, where they
live on the seabed. A few kinds are known from only
one specimen, and it is likely that more will be
discovered in the future.

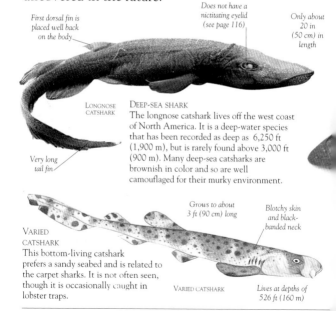

*First dorsal fin is
placed well back
on the body*

*Does not have a
nictitating eyelid
(see page 116)*

*Only about
20 in
(50 cm) in
length*

LONGNOSE
CATSHARK

*Very long
tail fin*

DEEP-SEA SHARK
The longnose catshark lives off the west coast
of North America. It is a deep-water species
that has been recorded as deep as 6,250 ft
(1,900 m), but is rarely found above 3,000 ft
(900 m). Many deep-sea catsharks are
brownish in color and so are well
camouflaged for their murky environment.

*Grows to about
3 ft (90 cm) long*

*Blotchy skin
and black-
banded neck*

VARIED
CATSHARK

This bottom-living catshark
prefers a sandy seabed and is related to
the carpet sharks. It is not often seen,
though it is occasionally caught in
lobster traps.

VARIED CATSHARK

*Lives at depths of
526 ft (160 m)*

TEETH

Swell sharks have wide mouths lined with a large number of tiny, sharp teeth. Their main food is small fish and bait used for catching lobster.

SWELL SHARK TEETH

GULF CATSHARK

In some species, females keep their egg cases inside their bodies until the young are nearly ready to hatch. This shark lives in the sea south of Australia.

Dense color with white spots

SWELL PROTECTION

The swell shark is nocturnal. It rests in crevices or among giant kelp during the day. If disturbed, it swallows water or air, and swells out its body to about twice its normal size. This makes it almost impossible to pull from its hiding place.

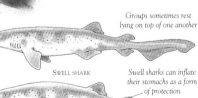

Groups sometimes rest lying on top of one another

SWELL SHARK

Swell sharks can inflate their stomachs as a form of protection

PLANKTON EATERS

THE THREE LARGEST FISH in the sea – the whale shark, basking shark, and megamouth shark – are all harmless, docile creatures that feed mainly on plankton. All have more than a thousand gill rakers that strain the current for food and an immense liver that contains a substantial amount of oil.

SEA SOUP
Plankton is made up of floating plants and animals that are unable to swim against the ocean currents. A few of these animals, such as jellyfish may be big, but most are tiny. Some, such as the larvae of crabs and sea urchins, are only part of the plankton "soup" for a short time before growing into adult animals.

PLANKTON

Copepod

Young fish

Copepod

BASKING SHARK

GENTLE GIANT
Basking sharks can measure more than 33 ft (10 m) in length and weigh more than 6 tons (6 tonnes). They are called "basking sharks" because they look as if they are sunbathing as they slowly swim on the surface filtering food.

INSIDE THE MOUTH

Basking sharks use the same action to feed and to breathe. Bars of cartilage in the throat support the gills and gill rakers. Water flows into the mouth, where it is strained through the gill rakers to filter out food particles. It is then pushed over the gills, where oxygen and carbon dioxide are exchanged.

BASKING SHARK

Copepod

Crab larva

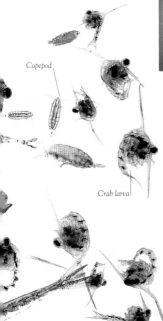

FOOD SIEVE

Each comblike gill raker is made of keratin, a material similar to human fingernails. Basking sharks may shed their gill rakers in winter and stop feeding, but since the sharks stay out of sight in deep water at this time, we cannot be sure.

GILL RAKERS OF A BASKING SHARK

Whale and megamouth shark

Whale and megamouth sharks are plankton
eaters that live in tropical waters. Both are
enormous: the whale shark is the largest of
all fish and may grow to a length of 59 ft
(18 m) and weigh up to 44 tons (40 tonnes).
The megamouth measures more than 13 ft (4 m).
Anatomically, the megamouth is more closely
related to the great white
than to other
filter feeders.

OPEN WIDE
The whale shark's mouth is small
compared with that of a basking
shark. The gill arches are connected
by gristly bars that support mesh filters
that trap plankton.

*Open mouth of the
whale shark*

TINY TEETH
Whale sharks have a large
number of tiny teeth that serve
no function since they cannot
chew or tear food. However,
divers can be bruised if an arm or
a leg becomes caught on the
shark's teeth.

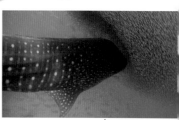

WHALE SHARK TEETH

ANCESTRAL BEHAVIOR
Whale sharks have been observed more or less
vertical in the water when feeding on small
fish such as anchovies. This unusual feeding
posture probably harks back to the
habits of their ancient ancestors.

8 4

PLACID GIANTS
Despite their size, whale sharks are harmless and can be
closely approached by divers. Unfortunately, this also
means that they make easy targets for hunters in some
tropical island communities, who harpoon them.
Their fins are sold to make soup.

*Longer upper
lobe of tail*

*Silvery luminescence around the
mouth is thought to attract
shrimps and other food*

NEW SPECIES
The megamouth shark escaped the
attention of science until 1976 when one
was accidentally caught off the coast of
Hawaii by a US research vessel. It was
hauled aboard so scientists could
examine the specimen in detail.

MEGAMOUTH SHARK

DEEP-SEA DWELLERS

THE AVERAGE DEPTH of the oceans is about 11,500 ft (3,500 m). Most of this vast bulk of water is cold, and largely unknown. There is no light in the oceans below 3,300 ft (1,000 m), and at these depths, fish tend to be small because food is scarce. Many species use light signals to communicate with one another, to lure prey, or to find a mate.

BLACKBELLY LANTERN SHARK

BLACKBELLY LANTERN SHARK
Lantern sharks have been found at depths of 6,500 ft (2,000 m). Like most deep-water fish, they have large eyes to make use of what little light there may be. They emit a bright green glow from light-producing organs along their flanks.

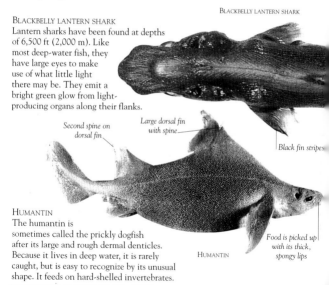

Second spine on dorsal fin

Large dorsal fin with spine

Black fin stripes

HUMANTIN
The humantin is sometimes called the prickly dogfish after its large and rough dermal denticles. Because it lives in deep water, it is rarely caught, but is easy to recognize by its unusual shape. It feeds on hard-shelled invertebrates.

HUMANTIN

Food is picked up with its thick, spongy lips

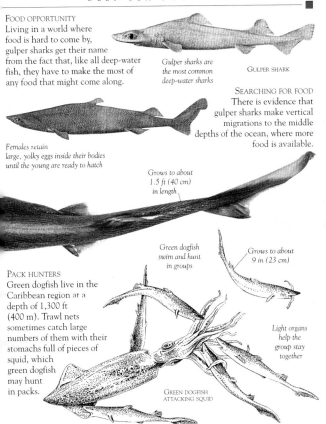

FOOD OPPORTUNITY
Living in a world where food is hard to come by, gulper sharks get their name from the fact that, like all deep-water fish, they have to make the most of any food that might come along.

Gulper sharks are the most common deep-water sharks

GULPER SHARK

SEARCHING FOR FOOD
There is evidence that gulper sharks make vertical migrations to the middle depths of the ocean, where more food is available.

Females retain large, yolky eggs inside their bodies until the young are ready to hatch

Grows to about 1.5 ft (40 cm) in length

Green dogfish swim and hunt in groups

Grows to about 9 in (23 cm)

PACK HUNTERS
Green dogfish live in the Caribbean region at a depth of 1,300 ft (400 m). Trawl nets sometimes catch large numbers of them with their stomachs full of pieces of squid, which green dogfish may hunt in packs.

Light organs help the group stay together

GREEN DOGFISH ATTACKING SQUID

STRANGE SHARKS

SOME OF THE MOST UNUSUAL sharks live in rarely
explored habitats. Some species are known by only
one or two specimens, so their behavior can only
be guessed at. Sometimes there may be clues, such
as the curious wounds in the bodies of seals and
whales – which turned out to be
the work of the cookie-
cutter shark.

ODD BITE

Cookie-cutters are only 20 in
(50 cm) long, yet they have
the largest teeth, compared
with their size, of any living
shark. They feed by gouging
round plugs of flesh from their victims.

*Flexible lips clamp
onto prey*

*Disk-shaped bite
from cookie-cutter*

COOKIE-CUTTER

*This dwarf shark is only
about 6 in (15 cm) long*

*It is protected by a
spine on its first
dorsal fin*

DWARF SHARK

The dwarf shark is known
from very few specimens.
It lives in deep
water, in the
Pacific Ocean. It
seems likely that it
makes vertical
migrations, as it has
also been caught in shallow
seas. Like many deep-sea fish, it
has light organs on its underside.

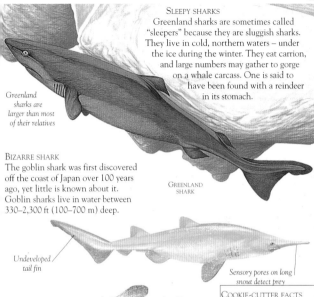

SLEEPY SHARKS

Greenland sharks are sometimes called "sleepers" because they are sluggish sharks. They live in cold, northern waters – under the ice during the winter. They eat carrion, and large numbers may gather to gorge on a whale carcass. One is said to have been found with a reindeer in its stomach.

Greenland sharks are larger than most of their relatives

GREENLAND SHARK

BIZARRE SHARK

The goblin shark was first discovered off the coast of Japan over 100 years ago, yet little is known about it. Goblin sharks live in water between 330–2,300 ft (100–700 m) deep.

Undeveloped tail fin

Sensory pores on long snout detect prey

UNDERSIDE OF HEAD

TOP SIDE OF HEAD

The goblin, or "elfin," shark grows to about 13 ft (4 m) in length

Its flabby body suggests an inactive lifestyle

COOKIE-CUTTER FACTS

• Cookie-cutters were named after the cookie-shaped bite they leave on their victims.

• Cookie-cutters are one of the few sharks that attack prey much larger than themselves.

SHARK ODDITIES

SHARKS ARE SUPREME evolutionary
opportunists, filling all kinds of roles and
thriving in almost all marine habitats.
Some even mimic the appearance
– and success – of other fish,
such as rays and sawfish, but
beneath their sometimes
strange surface appearance,
the true structure of the
shark remains.

Equal-sized teeth

SAWFISH
TEETH

STARRY RAY
Rays have cartilaginous
skeletons and dermal denticles like sharks,
but have followed a separate evolutionary
path since the time of the dinosaurs.
The starry ray lives on the seabed in
cold waters around the coasts
of Europe and eastern
North America.

SAWFISH
Sawfish are
related to rays
but have long,
flattened snouts like
sawsharks. Sawfish teeth
are all the same size,
unlike those of sawsharks,
which differ in length.
Sawfish grow to more
than 33 ft (10 m)
in length.

Sawshark teeth are different sizes

SAWSHARK
Sawsharks stir up the
seabed with their long,
toothed snout, feeling
for small fish and crabs with their
barbels. Baby sawsharks' teeth are
covered with skin up to the time they
are born, so they don't injure their
mother or one another.

WELL
HIDDEN
An angel shark is hard to see as it
lies on the seabed. Its body is so flat that
it appears no more than a low mound in
the sand. Unlike a ray, it uses its tail
rather than its large fins to swim.

ANGEL SHARK

Mouth at
front
of head

ANGEL SHARK
There are 13 different kinds of angel
shark and all live in shallow, warm
seas, though some migrate to warmer
waters during the summer. They
hunt at night in their own
territories. Unlike rays, they
have sharp teeth for feeding on
shelled prey and small fish.

Large
pectoral
fin

Sandy-colored skin is
well camouflaged for
life on the seabed

UNDER THE SAND
Angel sharks
disguise themselves
by covering their
bodies in sand.

Angel shark
covers itself
in sand

ODDITIES FACTS

• Angel shark is often
sold as a substitute for
shrimp or lobster.

• Like a ray, an angel
shark has eyes on the
top of its head so it can
see while lying flat.

• The body length of
Sawfish is ten times
longer than sawsharks.

EVOLUTIONARY LEFTOVERS

TODAY'S SEAS provide an environment similar to that of the ancient oceans in which sharks evolved. Some sharks have become extinct, their places taken by more efficient species, but others have survived unchanged for millions of years. Several species were known only to science from fossils before the living animals were found.

SEVEN-GILLED SHARK
Some rare sharks have six or even seven gill openings. The way the jaws are attached to the skull, and the fact that there is little calcium hardening their vertebrae makes them similar to primitive sharks.

SEVEN-GILLED SHARK

Grows to almost 7 ft (2 m) in length

Eel-like body shape

LIVING FOSSIL
More than any other shark, the frilled shark can be called a living fossil. It has six gill slits, the first of which is very long and looks like a frilly collar. It is almost eel-like in shape, and many of its features and are not found in modern sharks. Scientists think that this species has the longest gestation period of any shark, at 2 or 3 years.

FRILLED SHARK

Spine

SPINE PROTECTION
The Port Jackson shark rests
during the day and hunts at
night, using its powerful
sense of smell to find food.
The large spine on its dorsal
fin protects it from being
swallowed by angel and wobbegong
sharks that lie in ambush.

PORT JACKSON
SHARK

HORN FOSSIL
The earliest fossil of a horn shark dates back
about 150 million years. Today, similar sharks
feed on shelled prey, which they crush with flat-
topped teeth much like those of ancient fossils.

DEEP-SEA HUNTER
The frilled shark is armed
with about 300 teeth, set in
27 rows. Each tooth carries
three sharp hooks, so prey
stand little chance of escape.

FRILLED SHARK TEETH

EVOLUTIONARY FACTS
• Frilled sharks are
found in deep water
throughout the world,
but are not common
anywhere.

• Horn sharks use fin
spines to burrow under
rocks, searching for prey.
The spines may wear
down to half their length.

SHARKS FOR THE FUTURE

DIVERSITY IN THE SEA

SINCE ANCIENT TIMES, sharks have been part of almost every marine environment, but today many species are threatened. Many people ask why the oceans need dangerous creatures such as sharks, but being major predators, sharks play an important role in preserving the balance of nature in the sea.

ABUNDANT SPECIES
There are more kinds of catshark than any other group of sharks, yet most of them are unfamiliar. They are usually small, few measuring more than 3 ft (1 m) in length, and often live on the seabed.

GULF
CATSHARK

INDISCRIMINATE EATERS
The bull shark, alone among present-day sharks, regularly enters the freshwater of estuaries and rivers. It thus comes into regular contact with humans and can be dangerous. It will eat almost any flesh, fresh or carrion, and is also attracted to waste thrown into rivers.

ANGLING FOR TROUBLE

The mako shark is an aggressive predator of tuna and mackerel, and a popular catch for sea anglers because of its fighting spirit and tasty flesh. This contact with anglers has provoked many attacks on humans.

The narrow teeth grab large fish that are swallowed whole

DIVERSITY FACTS

• Among them, sharks are able to feed on almost all creatures found in the sea.

• Over 340 species of sharks are known, but there may be more deep-water species to be found.

MAKO SHARK

BIG FISH

The largest of all fish, the whale shark sifts plankton from the sea with its gill rakers. It also eats small fish, which enables its worn gill rakers to regrow. It is possible that another plankton-feeder, the basking shark, hibernates to renew its gill rakers.

The whale shark has a smaller mouth than other plankton eaters

WHALE SHARK

SMALLEST SHARK

The lantern shark is the smallest of all sharks. It has been recorded at depths of 6,600 ft (2,000 m). Finding food and a mate is difficult at these cold, dark depths, but its light organs may help with both vital activities. It is possible that it hunts in groups.

SOUTHERN LANTERN SHARK

ENDANGERED SHARKS

SOME SPECIES of shark are rare because of exploitation by humans. All sharks breed slowly, some producing no more than two young a year, and many mature slowly, so that a depleted population cannot recover quickly.

LEFT TO DIE
Many sharks are seriously injured by game fishermen who hunt them for sport and leave them to die on the seafloor. Sometimes the fins are cut off a live shark to be sold. The body is then thrown back into the sea to die. In some parts of the West Indies and the Australian coast, the seabed is littered with corpses.

ENDANGERED YOUNG
Female sharks are larger than males, which makes them sought after by trophy hunters. Some species, such as blue sharks, swim into inshore waters to give birth. For every female caught, a litter of young has been lost – something that no animal species can withstand for long.

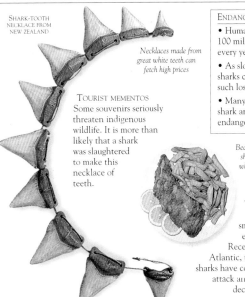

SHARK-TOOTH
NECKLACE FROM
NEW ZEALAND

*Necklaces made from
great white teeth can
fetch high prices*

TOURIST MEMENTOS
Some souvenirs seriously
threaten indigenous
wildlife. It is more than
likely that a shark
was slaughtered
to make this
necklace of
teeth.

ENDANGERED FACTS
• Humans kill up to
100 million sharks
every year.
• As slow breeders,
sharks cannot replace
such losses.
• Many species of
shark are already
endangered.

*Because of overfishing,
sharks are now rare
where they were once
abundant*

UNDER ATTACK
The spiny dogfish
is one of many
small sharks caught
each year for food.
Recently in the North
Atlantic, the larger oceanic
sharks have come under similar
attack and have drastically
declined in numbers.

PRICELESS JAWS
Despite their high price, shark jaws are
popular with tourists, who severely
endanger the shark population by
buying them. However, attitudes may
be changing: for example, a recent
study in the Maldives estimated that a
living gray reef shark could generate
$2,500 in tourism. The same shark
dead would fetch only $24.

INDUSTRY

THE KILLING OF SHARKS for industrial use has a long history, since almost half the known species of shark have some commercial value. In the past, sharks' teeth were used as weapons, their skin was used as sandpaper, and their livers for oil. Today they are still hunted, but numbers are now in serious decline.

HAMMERHEAD TRAPPED IN NET

FISHING NETS
Sharks can easily become trapped in fishing nets used by trawlers or safety nets used to protect bathing beaches. Once entangled, it is almost impossible for them to escape. They often end up suffocating because they cannot keep water flowing over their gills.

ENVIRONMENTAL POLLUTION
Some sharks have been found with plastic packaging straps caught around their bodies. As the shark grows, the plastic gradually cuts into its flesh, resulting in horrible injuries to its body.

Because sharks cannot swim backward, they are unable to free themselves from packing straps that become caught around their bodies

LIVER PILLS
Health pills made from shark's liver claim to
reduce the incidence of heart disease and
cancer, and to increase longevity. For many
years, shark livers were used as a source
of vitamins A and E until a synthetic
alternative was discovered in the 1950's.

*Shark-fin
fibers look
like noodles*

SHARK-FIN SOUP

ASIAN DELICACY
Shark-fin soup is made from the
cartilaginous fibers in the fin of a
shark. After the fins are cut from
the shark and hung to dry, they
are soaked and repeatedly boiled
to extract the fibers. Other
ingredients are added to the
soup to give it flavor.

*Plastic that
has cut into
the shark's
body*

*Tiger, dusky,
and bull sharks
have been found off
the coast of Florida badly
injured by plastic straps*

COSMETICS
The gallbladder
and part of the
shark's liver have been
shown to improve acne and
other skin complaints.
However, natural plant oils are
just as effective for improving
these skin conditions.

INDUSTRY FACTS
• As it becomes more
affordable, shark-fin
soup is increasing in
popularity throughout
the world.

• Drift nets used to
catch squid in the
North Pacific also
catch about 1.8 million
blue sharks each year.

TOURISM

ECOTOURISM, one of the fastest-growing tourism markets, could well be the key to some sharks' long-term survival. Sharks, swimming free in their own habitat, offer enormous economic potential as a tourist attraction.

SHARK PHOTOGRAPHY
Professional shark photographers often work from the protection of an underwater cage, particularly when filming a dangerous shark such as the great white. As a service for tourists, underwater safaris could give amateurs similar shelter and excitement.

Tail fluke of sperm whale off the coast of New Zealand

WHALE APPEAL
Whale watching is a valuable part of ecotourism. In some countries, it is now a bigger industry than hunting ever was. It is possible that shark-watching trips may also become a tourist attraction. Sharks are easily attracted using bait and unlike whales are less likely to be upset or distressed by the presence of humans.

IN THE RING
There are places where shark wrestling is staged as an attraction for tourists. While it apparently does little damage to the shark, it is one of the least desirable activities concerning tourism and sharks.

SHARK DIVES
Swimming with sharks is an exciting experience for the adventurous. Specialized tour operators can organize dives with hammerhead, reef, whale, and blue sharks – even the great white (which must be viewed from the safety of a strong cage).

MARINE AQUARIUM
Most aquariums show only small sharks, as big oceanic sharks are difficult to keep in captivity. The only great white ever kept in an aquarium had to be released after it repeatedly banged into the walls of its pool and became disoriented.

SHARKS IN SCIENCE

IN LABORATORIES in many parts of the world, teams of scientists are grappling with the intricacies of shark life, anatomy, and biochemistry. Much research centers on the fact that sharks appear to be unusually disease-free. The shark's physiological secrets may prove of great benefit to humankind.

DENTICLE RESEARCH
In the past, a shark's dermal denticles have provided information about teeth and their formation. More recently, scientists have come to believe that a shark's denticles move to affect water flow over its body. This may have potential applications in the field of ship and aircraft design.

DENTICLES
X 110 MAGNIFICATION

Ridges on the denticles help reduce drag

MONEY-SAVER
Tiny grooves on the dermal denticles of sharks such as hammerheads can reduce drag by up to 10 percent. Scientists are studying how these grooves work as a reduction in drag of only 1 or 2 percent could save the airline industry billions of dollars in fuel costs, as well as helping engineers design safer planes.

ANTIBIOTIC BREAKTHROUGH

Shark liver is a rich source of a steroid called squalamine. Its chief value seems to be as an antibiotic that may protect patients against bacteria, fungi, and other disease-causing organisms. It could also be useful in attacking bacteria that have become resistant to other drugs.

ARTIFICIAL SKIN

Here, in a medical laboratory, artificial skin grown from shark-fin cartilage is being used as a graft to heal a serious burn. Squalamine will increase its chance of success.

CURE FOR DISEASE

Besides being caught for food in large numbers, the spiny dogfish has contributed to our understanding of salt removal from the bloodstream. The mechanism that it employs to do this is proving useful as a way of treating the disease cystic fibrosis.

SPINY DOGFISH

SCIENCE FACTS

• Shark gallbladders have been used in the treatment of acne.

• Liver oil is still used in some cosmetics.

• Corneas from the eyes of sharks are used in some human transplant operations.

RESEARCH

ALTHOUGH HUMANS have had contact with sharks since prehistoric times, most research into their behavior is comparatively recent. Work with living sharks is concerned mainly with lifespan and migrations; it usually involves tagging or radio-tracking individuals for a short time.

TAGGING SHARKS

Baited hooks are used to catch a shark

The shark is carefully brought on board

REELING IN
A shark must be caught before it can be tagged. Most tagging is done by game fishermen who record the weight and size of the shark on special cards issued by research institutions.

TAGGING
The tag, which is a noncorrosive numbered disk or dart, is placed securely in the muscles just below the first dorsal fin. Should the shark be caught again in another part of the world, there is an address on the reverse side of the tag where it can be returned.

RELEASE
Once tagged, the shark is returned to the sea. If it is caught again, the catcher should inform the tagging authority so that information about the shark can be recorded and exchanged.

326

ATLANTIC SHARK MOVEMENTS

SHARK MOVEMENTS OFF AUSTRALIA

OCEAN MOVEMENTS

Few sharks are recovered, but some are known to have lived for as long as 20 years after they were tagged. These maps show shark movements tracked as a result of tagging on the east coasts of the US and Australia. Apart from the Port Jackson shark, the species tagged are fairly large and active. Small and deep-water sharks do not feature in these studies since they are hard to catch and follow.

SHARK KEY

WHALER	
HAMMERHEAD	
SANDBAR	
TIGER	
PORT JACKSON	
MAKO	

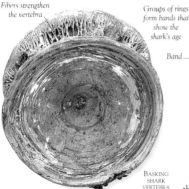

Fibers strengthen the vertebra

Groups of rings form bands that show the shark's age

Band

BASKING SHARK VERTEBRA

AGE RINGS

Sharks continue to grow throughout their lives, usually with seasonal spurts of growth. Scientists can assess the age and growth rates of sharks by treating the bones (vertebrae) of their backs with special chemicals.

PROTECTION

THE LARGE-SCALE destruction of sharks, mainly in the second half of this century, has led ecologists to pressure governments to protect both it and its environment. Despite opposition in some quarters, the killing of sharks is now controlled in many parts of the world.

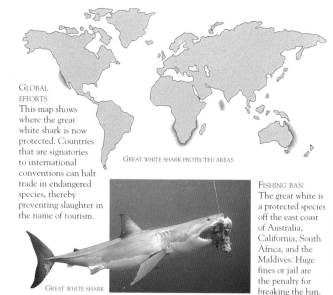

GLOBAL EFFORTS
This map shows where the great white shark is now protected. Countries that are signatories to international conventions can halt trade in endangered species, thereby preventing slaughter in the name of tourism.

GREAT WHITE SHARK PROTECTED AREAS

FISHING BAN
The great white is a protected species off the east coast of Australia, California, South Africa, and the Maldives. Huge fines or jail are the penalty for breaking the ban.

GREAT WHITE SHARK

EXTINCT SPECIES

Hybodus was a common shark alive during the time of the dinosaurs, yet about 65 million years ago, it became extinct. However, *Hybodus* disappeared gradually as modern sharks evolved. Today, wanton killing of sharks by humans leaves no time for replacement.

Hybodus had a large spine in front of both its dorsal fins

ACHILL ISLAND FISHERY STATISTICS

The table shows the decline in the numbers of basking shark caught off the Irish coast over a 20-year period. Fifty years ago the sight of a large school was commonplace. Now, owing to drastic over-exploitation it is no longer. The basking shark is a protected species around the British coast.

YEAR	NUMBER OF SHARKS TAKEN	TONS (TONNES) OF OIL SOLD
1951	1,630	375 (340)
1953	1,068	230 (209)
1955	1,708	135 (122)
1957	468	104 (94)
1959	280	70 (64)
1961	258	59 (54)
1963	75	19 (17)
1965	47	12 (11)
1967	41	11 (10)
1969	113	29 (26)
1971	29	7 (6)
1973	85	19 (17)
1975	38	9 (8)

PROTECTED SPECIES

After the late 1940's, when basking sharks were killed by harpoons with explosive heads, numbers declined drastically. Basking sharks are slow breeders and though they are now protected, it will be a long time before large numbers build up again.

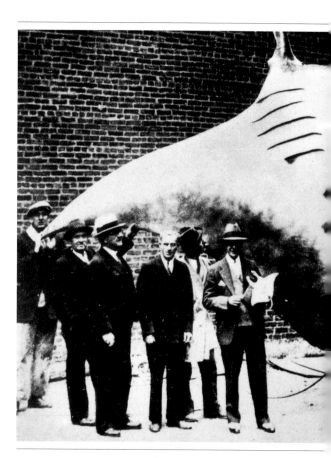

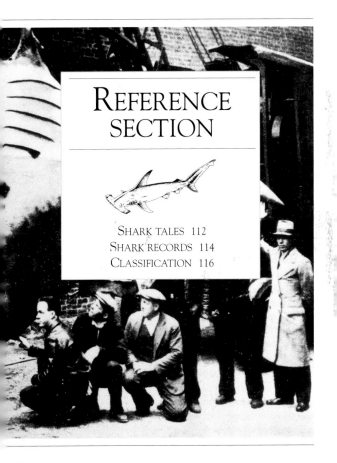

REFERENCE
SECTION

SHARK TALES

SHARKS ARE AMAZING animals but difficult to study, so little is known about them. Many stories are told by sailors, islanders, and fishermen – anyone who encounters a shark usually has a tale to tell. The more we know and understand, the more we can learn to respect such misunderstood creatures.

RARE SPECIES
The megamouth was accidentally discovered in 1976, and only three specimens have since been recorded. Another four specimens have reportedly been found but have not been officially documented.

MEGAMOUTH

SINKING SHIP
At the end of World War II, *Indianapolis*, the ship that carried part of the Hiroshima atomic bomb was torpedoed by a Japanese submarine. Of the 883 people who died, most fell victim to sharks, which attacked the survivors for four days until help arrived.

DEADLY TAIL
A sailor is reported to have been decapitated by the tail of a thresher in the Atlantic. Fishermen must be particularly careful of the thresher's powerful tail as it is almost the same length as its body. The thresher shark is a prized catch. Its spectacular leaps out of the water make it a challenge to land on board .

BIZARRE SHARK
The goblin shark is one of the oddest-looking sharks. It was discovered off the coast of Japan, but was first known from fossil teeth about 100 million years old. The goblin or elfin shark is a deep-water species, coloured pink with a brownish tint.

GOBLIN SHARK

GREAT WHITE SHARK

PERSISTENT JAWS
In 1966, a very persistent great white bit the leg of a teenage boy at a surfing beach south of Sydney, Australia. The lifesavers who rescued the boy were stunned to realize that they would have to lift the body of the shark out of the water as well, as it refused to let go. It was not until the shark had been beaten over the head repeatedly that it opened its jaws. Amazingly, the boy's leg was saved.

GOURMET DELIGHT
The poisonous flesh of the Greenland shark has a strong taste of ammonia, but is considered a delicacy in Iceland. The flesh is dried for several months before it is eaten. A strong, alcoholic local brew is served with the pieces of shark.

FOLLOW YOUR NOSE
Sharks have a remarkable sense of smell. Lemon sharks, under laboratory conditions, were found to be able to detect the scent of one part tuna fish to 25 million parts seawater. The hungrier the shark, the better its ability to detect the smell of fish in the water.

SLIM CHANCES
In Hawaii, the chance of drowning is more than 1,000 times greater than that of dying from a shark attack. In South Africa, the chance is 600 to 1, and in Australia, it is 50 to 1. However, bees kill more people in Australia each year than sharks do, while more people in the United States are killed by lightning than by sharks.

SOLVING THE PUZZLE
In the 1980's, the US Navy was baffled by disk-shaped bites in the rubber coating of the listening devices on their submarines. By accident, a whale and shark expert was shown the bite marks, which he immediately identified as being those of the little cookiecutter shark.

ANCIENT SHARK
The frilled shark is much the same as sharks that lived 20 million years ago and is the most primitive living species. Its broad-based, pointed teeth are found only in fossil sharks.

The female bears live young, producing 6–12 pups per litter

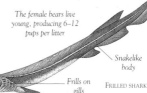

Snakelike body

Frills on gills

FRILLED SHARK

SHARK RECORDS

EVER SINCE HUMANS first ventured into the water, sharks have fascinated everyone who has encountered them. They come in many shapes and sizes and are indeed remarkable creatures. Scientists are still discovering new information about their biology and behavior much of which is still unknown.

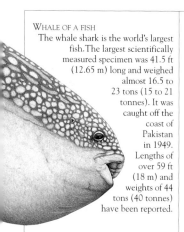

WHALE OF A FISH

The whale shark is the world's largest fish. The largest scientifically measured specimen was 41.5 ft (12.65 m) long and weighed almost 16.5 to 23 tons (15 to 21 tonnes). It was caught off the coast of Pakistan in 1949. Lengths of over 59 ft (18 m) and weights of 44 tons (40 tonnes) have been reported.

BABY NUMBERS

The gestation period for sharks varies from nine to 22 months. The number of pups born at any one time ranges from one to 100.

OLDER THAN THE DINOSAURS

In terms of animal evolution, sharks are true survivors. They have probably changed less than any other type of vertebrate. One of the oldest fish fossil found so far is of a jawless, armored fish called *Arandaspis*, discovered in central Australia. It has been dated to the Ordovician period, almost 500 million years ago.

SMALLEST SIZE

The spined pygmy shark is the world's smallest shark, measuring no more than 10 in (25 cm) long. It lives in deep tropical waters. It has a spine on its first dorsal fin and is luminescent only on its underside, making it hard for predators swimming above to spot.

GREAT WHITE

LONGEST DISTANCE

The blue is the greatest shark traveler. It has been tracked migrating distances of close to 3,726 miles (6,000 km) but mostly travels distances of about 1,550 miles (2,500 km). The mako, tiger, and sandbar sharks are all long-distance swimmers.

BLUE SHARK

FASTEST SWIMMERS

The blue shark and the mako shark are the fastest sharks. When catching food, the blue shark may accelerate to speeds of up to 43 mph (69 km/h). It is not possible for sharks to sustain high speeds, and most rarely exceed 7 mph (11 km/h). The fastest fish in the sea is the sailfish which can reach 68 mph (110 km/h).

MOST ABUNDANT SHARK

The spiny dogfish is one of the most common species found throughout the world. It is also the most widely eaten species and is fished in large numbers.

MOST DANGEROUS

Although the great white is the most feared of all sharks, the bull shark is actually responsible for the most attacks on humans. Hammerheads and tiger sharks are also responsible for many attacks. The sharks that are a threat to people tend to be more than 7 ft (2 m) in length. Because of its gruesome reputation, the great white has become endangered, and in some countries it is now a protected species.

JAWS

Peter Benchley's novel *Jaws*, about a killer great white menacing residents of an American vacation resort, is one of the world's best-selling fiction titles. The first Hollywood movie based on the book has become one of the top-grossing films of all time, spawning three sequels, including a 3-D version in which the shark seems to shoot right out of the screen.

SPINED PYGMY SHARK

This pygmy shark is actual size, and measures only 5 in (13 cm) long

CLASSIFICATION

ANIMALS ARE CLASSIFIED into groups that share similar characteristics. Sharks are divided into eight orders. Each order contains families, which include genera and species. Only members of the same species can breed with one another.

Anal fin present

Two dorsal fins, five gill openings

No spines on dorsal fin

Spines on dorsal fin

Large mouth behind eyes

Small mouth in front of eyes

Nictitating eyelid

No nictitating eyelid

CARCHARHINI-
FORMES
The biggest group includes large sharks such as the requiems and hammerheads.

LAMNIFORMES
Large, fast-swimming sharks includes the mackerel, basking, goblin, thresher, and mako sharks.

ORECTOLOBIFORMES
This group lives in shallow water and includes the nurse, whale, zebra, bamboo, and wobbegong sharks.

HETERODONTI-
FORMES
Bottom-living, eat hard-shelled food, such as clams and crabs: horn and Port Jackson sharks.

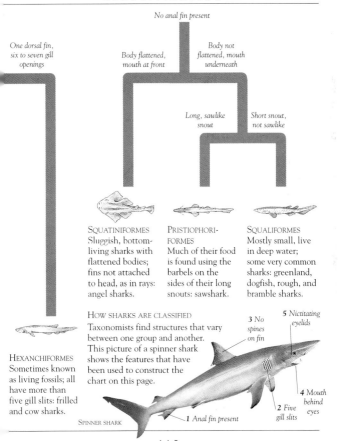

No anal fin present

One dorsal fin, six to seven gill openings

Body flattened, mouth at front

Body not flattened, mouth underneath

Long, sawlike snout

Short snout, not sawlike

SQUATINIFORMES
Sluggish, bottom-living sharks with flattened bodies; fins not attached to head, as in rays: angel sharks.

PRISTIOPHORI-FORMES
Much of their food is found using the barbels on the sides of their long snouts: sawshark.

SQUALIFORMES
Mostly small, live in deep water; some very common sharks: greenland, dogfish, rough, and bramble sharks.

HEXANCHIFORMES
Sometimes known as living fossils; all have more than five gill slits: frilled and cow sharks.

HOW SHARKS ARE CLASSIFIED
Taxonomists find structures that vary between one group and another. This picture of a spinner shark shows the features that have been used to construct the chart on this page.

3 No spines on fin

5 Nictitating eyelids

4 Mouth behind eyes

2 Five gill slits

1 Anal fin present

SPINNER SHARK

117

Resources

PLACES WHERE YOU CAN SEE SHARKS

The best place to see sharks in the wild is the tropics. Alternatively, most aquariums have shark exhibits, and some even allow visitors to touch sharks and rays. Here is a sampling of aquariums, all of which have educational and conservation programs as well as viewing tanks or larger displays.

New York Aquarium
Surf Avenue and
West 8th Street
Brooklyn, NY 11224
The aquarium has a 90,000-gallon shark tank containing sharks and rays. Visitors can watch the daily shark feeding.

Mote Marine Laboratory
1600 Ken Thompson Pkwy.
Sarasota, FL 34236
The center for Shark Research has an aquarium where sharks of the region are displayed.

John G. Shedd Aquarium
1200 South Lake Shore Dr.
Chicago, IL 60605
The exhibit "Wild Reef" shows 26 different habitats and more than 30 sharks. The Caribbean coral reef exhibit hosts bonnethead sharks.

Monterey Bay Aquarium
886 Cannery Row
Monterey, CA 93940
This aquarium has exhibits on the animals that inhabit or visit the bay, and its tank re-creates the aquatic life of the bay.

National Aquarium in Baltimore
Pier 3
501 East Pratt Street
Baltimore, MD 21202
This aquarium has two shark exhibits called "Wings in the Water" and "The Open Ocean."

New England Aquarium
Central Wharf
Boston, MA 02110
In both the Giant Ocean Tank, a re-creation of a coral reef, and the smaller tanks, about five shark species are displayed. On the Touch Trolley are samples of shark teeth, shark skin, and other items for visitors.

Sea World
500 Sea World Drive
San Diego, CA 92109
In "Shark Encounter," visitors walk through a tube as they view rays and sharks—sandtiger, bonnethead, and others.

Sea World
7007 Sea World Drive
Orlando, FL 32821
Visitors walk down a 60-foot tunnel through a coral reef habitat that features sharks, eels, and barracudas.

Sea World
10500 Sea World Drive
San Antonio, TX 78251
An exhibit of a habitat in the Pacific and Indian oceans features sharks. Visitors can also watch the sharks being fed.

Seattle Aquarium
Pier 59
1483 Alaskan Way
Seattle, WA 98101
Sharks can be found
swimming with warm-
water fish in the Pacific
Coral Reef habitat, as well
as in the underwater
Dome exhibit.

ORGANIZATIONS
INTERESTED IN
SHARKS

**International Union for
the Conservation of
Nature (IUCN)**
Florida Museum of
Natural History
Dickinson Hall
Ichthyology Department
University of Florida
Gainesville, FL 32611
The IUCN Shark
Specialist Group is
composed of member
organizations who
promote worldwide shark
conservation and
management.

**Pelagic Shark Research
Foundation**
100 Shaffer Road
Santa Cruz, CA 95060

This nonprofit research
and educational group
works to foster better
understanding of sharks.

SOME SHARK
PUBLICATIONS

The Life of Sharks
Brudner, Paul. New York:
Columbia University
Press, 1972

*Sharks: Myth and
Reality*
Caffero, Gaetano, and
Maddelena Jahoda.
Charlottesville, VA:
Thomasson-Grant, 1994

The Book of Sharks
Ellis, Richard. New York:
Knopf, 1989

*Shark: Nature's
Masterpiece*
Lawrence, R. D. Shelburne,
VT: Chapters, 1994

*Sharks: The Perfect
Predators*
Hall, Howard. Rev. ed.
San Luis Obispo, CA:
Blake, 1993

Natural History of Sharks
Lineaweaver, T. H. III, and
R. H. Backus. New York:
Lyons and Burford, 1986

Shark
MacQuitty, Miranda.
New York: Knopf, 1992

World of Sharks
Palmer, Sarah, 6 vols.
New York: Random
House, 1990

*Sharks in Question: The
Smithsonian Answer Book*
V. G. Springer and J. P.
Gold, Washington, DC:
Smithsonian Institution
Press, 1989

*Sharks: Silent Hunters
of the Deep*
Introduction by R. and
V. Taylor, New York: DK
Publishing, Inc., 1991

Glossary

ADAPTATION
An evolutionary process that enables living things to fit their environment as perfectly as possible. An organ that develops in the uterus of some sharks for the nourishment of the embryo.

AMPULLAE OF LORENZINI
Pores around the snout and head of a shark that contain organs sensitive to weak electric charges in the water.

ANAL FIN
A small fin on the underside of a shark located near its tail.

BARBEL
A sensitive, fingerlike projection near the mouth of some sharks and other fish, which enables them to detect food hidden in mud or sand.

CARTILAGINOUS FISH
Fish that have skeletons formed of cartilage, not bone. They include sharks, skates, rays, chimeras, and banjo fish.

CAUDAL FIN
The tail fin.

CARTILAGE
A firm, gristly material that forms the skeletons of sharks. It is not as hard as bone, though it may be strengthened by calcium salts.

COMMENSAL
An animal that lives in association with a creature of a different species, like a pilot fish with a shark, but each is able to survive without the other.

COPEPOD
One of over 4,500 species of tiny animals – most less than 0.08 inches (2 mm) long – which are an important part of the plankton.

CORNEA
The thick but transparent skin that covers and protects the eyes of animals with backbones and octopuses and squids.

DENTINE
The chief material from which teeth are made.

It is made almost entirely from minerals.

DERMAL DENTICLES
"Skin teeth." These form an armor in a shark's skin. Denticles are made like teeth, with bony bases and an upper part of dentine, covered with enamel. Most dermal denticles have minute ridges, which help guide water over a shark's side so that it swims more efficiently.

DORSAL FIN
A fin on the midline of the back of a fish.

ECOLOGIST
A person who studies the environment.

ENAMEL
The hard covering to the exposed part of a tooth. It is the hardest part of an animal's body.

EMBRYO
A developing animal before it is born or hatched from an egg.

FEEDING FRENZY
The way that sharks compete for food,

regardless of their own safety, when there is blood or abundant food in the water.

FOSSIL
A plant or animal that lived long ago but became preserved in rock after it died.

GALLBLADDER
A small pouch attached to the liver, which stores a substance called bile. Bile has various functions, the most important of which is aiding the digestion of fat.

GESTATION
The period that an embryo takes to develop before birth.

GILL RAKER
A comblike organ growing from a gill arch of a fish, including some sharks. Its function is to strain tiny organisms from the water as it passes over the fish's gills.

GILLS
The breathing organs of fish through which oxygen is taken into the animal's body and waste carbon dioxide is

expelled into the water. In sharks and their relatives the gills are unprotected and can be seen as a series of between five and seven slits just behind the head.

INTERNEURALS
Part of the structure of a vertebra of a shark.

LATERAL LINE
A series of pressure-sensitive organs around the head and forming a line down the side of fish.

MIGRATION
Regular movement of an animal population from one area to another and back again, usually on a yearly basis.

NICTITATING MEMBRANE
Often called the third eyelid, the nictitating membrane moves across the surface of the eye to clean and protect it.

OLFACTORY
Concerning the sense of smell.

OVO-VIVIPAROUS
Reproduction where the young develop inside the body but when born, lack a placenta and rely on a yolk sac.

SHAGREEN
The dried skin of a shark. At one time used like sandpaper, for polishing marble and other hard substances.

TAPETUM
A layer of cells that lies behind the retina of some fish and nocturnal animals. It reflects light back into the eye, so that it is used most effectively in dim conditions.

VERTICAL MIGRATION
Movement of marine creatures from one level in the water to another. Many planktonic organisms make vertical migrations daily. They may be followed by fish and other predators.

VIVIPAROUS
Reproduction where the young stays in the mother's body until ready to be born.

Scientific names

A
African lantern shark
(*Etmopterus polli*)
Angel shark
(*Squatina squatina*)
Argentine angel shark
(*Squatina argentina*)

B
Basking shark
(*Cetorhinus maximus*)
Blackbelly lantern shark
(*Etmopterus lucifer*)
Blacktip reef shark
(*Carcharhinus melanopterus*)
Blue shark
(*Prionace glauca*)
Blue-spotted bamboo shark
(*Chiloscyllium caerulopunctatum*)
Bonnethead shark
(*Sphyrna tiburo*)
Bramble shark
(*Echinorhinus brucus*)
Brown-banded bamboo shark
(*Chiloscyllium punctatum*)
Brown-spotted catshark
(*Scyliorhinus garmani*)
Bull shark
(*Carcharhinus leucas*)

C
Caribbean reef shark
(*Carcharhinus perezi*)
Cookie-cutter shark
(*Isistius brasiliensis*)

D
Dwarf shark
(*Scyliorhinus torrei*)
Dumb gulper shark
(*Centrophorus harrissoni*)
Dusky catshark
(*Halaelurus canescens*)
Dusky shark
(*Carcharhinus obscurus*)

E
Epaulette shark
(*Hemiscyllium ocellatum*)

F
Freckled catshark
(*Scyliorhinus haeckli*)
Frilled shark
(*Chlamydoselachus anguineus*)

G
Goblin shark
(*Mitsukurina owstoni*)
Great white shark
(*Carcharodon carcharias*)
Green dogfish
(*Etmopterus virens*)
Greenland shark
(*Somniosus microcephalus*)
Gray reef shark
(*Carcharhinus amblyrhynchos*)
Gulf catshark
(*Asymbolus vincenti*)
Gulper shark
(*Centrophorus granulosus*)

H
Hooktooth dogfish
(*Aculeola nigra*)
Horn shark
(*Heterodontus francisci*)
Humantin
(*Oxynotus bruniensis*)

L
Lemon shark
(*Negaprion brevirostris*)
Leopard shark
(*Triakis semifasciata*)
Lesser spotted dogfish
(*Scyliorhinus caniculus*)
Longnose catshark
(*Apristurus kampae*)

M
Mako shark
(*Isurus oxyrhinchus*)
Manta ray
(*Aetobatus narinari*)
Megamouth shark
(*Megachasma pelagios*)

N
Nurse shark
(*Ginglymostoma cirratum*)

P
Pacific sleeper shark
(*Somniosus pacificus*)
Panama ghost shark
(*Apristurus stenseni*)
Plunket shark
(*Centroscymnus plunketi*)
Porbeagle
(*Lamna nasus*)
Portuguese dogfish
(*Centroscymnus coelolepis*)
Prickly dogfish (humantin)
(*Oxynotus bruniensis*)
Port Jackson shark
(*Heterodontus portusjacksoni*)

S
Sandbar shark
(*Carcharhinus plumbeus*)

Sandtiger shark
(*Carcharius taurus*)
Sawfish
(*Pristis spp.*)
Sawshark
(*Pristiophorus cirratus*)
Scalloped hammerhead shark
(*Sphyrna lewini*)
Seven-gilled shark
(*Notorhynchus cepidianus*)
Sharptooth houndshark
(*Triakis megalopterus*)
Silky shark
(*Carcharhinus falciformis*)
Slender bamboo shark
(*Chiloscyllium indicum*)
Smallbelly catshark
(*Apristurus indicus*)
Smooth-hound shark
(*Mustelus spp.*)
Spinner shark
(*Carcharhinus brevipinna*)
Spiny (piked) dogfish
(*Squalus acanthius*)
Spotted wobbegong
(*Orectolobus maculatus*)
Starry ray
(*Raja radiata*)

Swellshark
(*Cephaloscyllium ventriosum*)

T
Tassled wobbegong
(*Eucrossorhinus dasypogon*)
Thornback ray
(*Raja clavata*)
Thorny lantern shark
(*Etmopterus stensosus*)
Thresher shark
(*Alopias vulpinus*)
Tiger shark
(*Galeocerdo cuvier*)

V
Varied catshark
(*Parascyllium variolatum*)

W
Whale shark
(*Rhincodon typus*)
Whitenose shark
(*Nasolamia velox*)
Wobbegong
(*Orectolobus spp.*)

Z
Zebra shark
(*Stegostoma fasciatum*)
Zebra bullhead shark
(*Heterodontus zebra*)

Index

Acknowledgments

DK would like to thank:
Hilary Bird for the index; Caroline Potts for
picture library services; Louise Thomas for
picture research; Janet Allis, Karen Fielding,
and Clair Watson for design assistance, Natasha
Billing and Robert Graham for research
assistance, and Tony Chung for jacket design.

Illustrations by:
Janet Allis, Martin Camm, Peter Visscher,
Rolf Williams, and John Woodcock.

Photographs by:
Richard Davis, Michael Dent, Andrew
Einsiedel, Frank Greenway, Colin Keates, Dave
King, Tim Parmenter, Michael Pitts, Mike Row,
Harry Taylor, and John Williams

Picture credits:
t=top b=bottom c=center l=left r=right.
The publisher would like to thank the following
for their kind permission to reproduce their
photographs:
Ardea: 56tl, 60br, 60bl, 60tr, 61cl, B & P Boyle
84br, Kenneth W Fink 70bl, Ron and Valerie
Taylor 12b, Valerie Taylor 62tl, 63br, 63bl, 74c;
Bahamas Tourist Board: 103bl; BBC Natural
History Unit: Jeff Rotman 81t, Barbara Todd
102bl; Bridgeman Art Library: 63tl, 102tl; British
Museum, London: 65t, Bruce Coleman: Michael
Glover 83tr, Jeffrey L Rotman 52/3, 102cr; CM
Dixon: 64br; Mary Evans Picture Library: 55tr,
55cl, Ronald Grant Archive: 54cl, Institute of
Heraldic and Genealogical Studies, Canterbury:
63tr; FLPA: F Savastano/Panda 84cl, DP Wilson
36br; The London Sun: 13b; Museum of
Mankind, London: 97tl; Natural History Museum
London: 35tc; NHPA: 57tl, A.N.T. 108b, GI
Bernard 36c, Peter Parks 21br, Norbert Wu 33cr,
79br; Natural Science Photos: Bob Cranston 84cl,
98b, Nat Fain 113tl, David B Fleetham 88cr, Paul
Kay 44c; Oxford Scientific Films: 8/9c, 43br, Fred
Bavendam 100 cr, Tony Crabtree 30bl, Howard
Hall 22/3, 21t, 115cl, Rudie H Kuiter 81c, 86b,
Zig Leszczynski 75cl, Tom McHugh 33bl, Planet
Earth Pictures: 57br, 66/7, Kurt Amsler 96tr, Mark
Conlin 69bl, Ken Lucas 92cr, Doug Perrine 47 tl,
47cr, 97br, 98c, 99br, Peter Rollands 104bl, 109bl,
Warren Williams 103tr, Norbert Wu 94/5, 80c;
Joyce Pope: 45bl; Science Photo Library: Eye of
Science 105cr, Bsip Leca 105tr, Hank Morgan
105cl; Seapics.com/Chris Huss: 76-77b;
Smithsonian: T Britt Griswold 88bl; Vardon
Attractions: 103cl; Waterhouse: Stephen Frink
14cl, 100bl, Howard Hall 69c, James Watt 8/9c,
42c, 57c, 84t; Werner Forman Archive: British
Museum, London 64c, Field Museum of Natural
History, Chicago, US 65bc; Brad Wetherbee:
Gwen Lowe 86c, 93bc, 114br, Peter McMillan
101b; Wild Images: 40l, 61tr, Howard Hall 10/1,
21cl, 38/9, 48br, 49tr, 50br, 71tl, 101t, Louise
Murray 96b, Adrian Warren 62br.

Every effort has been made to trace the copyright
holders and we apologize in advance for any
unintentional omissions. We would be pleased to
insert the appropriate acknowledgment in any
subsequent edition of this publication.

All other images © Dorling Kindersley
For further information see:
www.dkimages.com